ENCYCLOPEDIA
OF
Window Fashions

t Illustrations
Cover Design
tricia Marovich

By Charles T. Randall

Introduction

THE ENCYCLOPEDIA OF WINDOW FASHIONS is the original book of it's kind. It's primary purpose is to make window decorating easier and more profitable for window covering professionals. It will also be useful for those looking for window decorating ideas, and information. Surprisingly, I was unable to find a similar book, after a long and ardent search. However, inspiration prevailed, and the adage rang in my ears . . . "Find a need and fill it." So here you have it! A window decorating book designed to make your presentations more professional. Designed to save you enormous time in preparing presentations, i.e., expressing creative ideas. And designed to help you find the best possible solution for the window.

Here are a few tips to help you get the most out of the book: (1) Have your customers read the bottom half of page five (the part about lining). The use of lining generally makes for a better product. (2) Offer them the more decorative window covering solutions. Example, a pleated arched valance, (V101), or a cloud on a continental rod, (V115). And always offer them accessories (Pg. 69) and so on. Also, do take some time and become familiar with the book. Sometimes you'll find the treatment you need in an unexpected solution or chapter. Example: addtional valance illustrations are in the DRAPERIES chapter, and in the CAFE AND CURTAIN STYLES chapter. Also, rod top and bottom illustrations are in both the WINDOWS WITH A CHALLENGE chapter, and in the R.T.B./TIE BANDS/ACCESSORIES chapter.

Here's an idea you may find helpful. Photocopy some of the pages containing your favorite treatments. Then color them in using a good set of watercolor pens. This will show your customers how enhancing contrasting banding, welting, or ruffles can be. And will add a real designer touch to your presentation.

Sincerely,

Charles Randall

Special Note:

This manual has been thoughtfully designed with numbers at the top right hand portion of the Illustration. Using these numbers will eliminate misunderstandings between designers, workrooms and installers.

Special thanks to Wesco Fabrics, Inc. and Fabricut-Trend.
Most illustrations by Patricia Marovich, Design Visuals, Fountain Valley, CA.

Glossary of Window Decorating Ter[ms]

A

"A" Frame Window — Very contemporary house structures sometimes forms an "A" shape. When draperies are used, they hang from the cross-beam of the "A," or they can be fabricated and installed to conform to the shape of the window.

Allowance — A customary variation from an "exact" measurement, taken for the purpose of anticipated needs.

Apron — A piece of wood trim beneath the window sill.

B

Bar-Tack — A sewing machine operation of repeated stitches concentrated to secure the lowest portion of drapery pleats.

Baton — A rod or wand used to hand draw traverse draperies.

Bay Window — A large projecting type of window made of a group of windows set at angles to each other and joined to each other on some sides.

Bottom Hem — The turned part forming a finished edge at bottom of drapery.

Bow Window — A large projecting type of window that is curved or semi-circular.

Box Pleat — A fold of cloth sewn into place to create fullness in a drapery. Box pleats are evenly spaced and stitched.

Bracket — Metal piece attached to the wall or casing to support a drapery or curtain rod.

C

Cafe — A traversing or non-traversing drapery, designed as a tier. The heading can be various styles. They can be set at a variety of heights to control ventilation, view and light.

Cafe Rod — A small, round decorative rod which comes in white, brass or woodgrain finish. Cafe rods are meant to be seen and add an additional decorative touch to the curtain treatment.

Canopy — A fabric window topper created by sewing pockets into fabric panels and inserting a rod with a small projection at the top of the panel, a rod with a larger projection at the bottom.

Cantonniere — A three-sided shaped or straight cornice that "frames" the window — across the top and down the two sides. It is made of a hardboard, padded and covered with fabric.

Carriers — Small runners installed in a traverse rod which hold a drapery pin or hook.

Cartridge Pleat — A fold of cloth sewn into place to create fullness in a drapery. This is a round pleat 2-2½ inches in depth. Roundness is created by stuffing of crinoline or paper (removed for cleaning).

Cascade — A fall of fabric that descends in a zig-zag line from a drapery heading or top treatment.

Casement — (1) A cloth drapery that is of an open-weave material but more opaque than a sheer. (2) A type of vertically hinged window, whose panes open by sliding sideways or cranking outward.

Casing (Window) — Wooden frame around a window.

Center Draw — One pair of draperies which draws open and closes exactly at a window's center point.

Center Support — A metal grip which is used to support a traverse rod from above and prevents rod from sagging in the middle, but does not interfere with rod operation.

Clerestory Windows — A series of small windows which let in light and air. These are placed high on the wall to allow complete privacy.

Corner Window — A corner window literally wraps [around the corner] of the building at right angles.

Cornice — A shallow, box-like structure, usually [of] wood, fastened across the top of a window to co[nceal] drapery hardware.

Crinoline — A heavily sized, stiff fabric used as a fo[rm] to support the edge of a hem or puffed sleeve. Also [called] interlining.

Custom-Made Draperies — Draperies made to o[rder in a] workroom or decorator shop.

Cut Length — The cut length of the fabric is the len[gth after] allowances have been made for heading and hem.

D

Dormer Window — A dormer window is an uprigh[t window] which breaks the surface of a sloping roof.

Double Hung — May be several items: Double hung [windows,] Double hung shutters, and Double hung draperies [(two sets] of draperies usually sheer fabric under opaque fab[ric, each] operating independently).

Draw Draperies — Panels of fabric, featuring [pleated] headings.

E

End Bracket — The two supporting metal grips wh[ich hold] a drapery rod to the wall or ceiling. They control th[e amount] of projection.

End Housing — Refers to the box parts at the extre[me ends] of a traverse drapery rod. They enclose the me[chanism] through which the cords run.

F

Fenestration — Location and proportion of win[dows in] relationship to solid wall areas.

Festoon — A decorative drapery treatment of fold[s of fabric] that hangs in a graceful curve, and frames the [top of a] window.

Finial — Decorative end piece on cafe rods or de[corative] traverse rods (also referred to as "pole ends").

Finished Length — This is the length after drape[ries have] been made, using the extra allowances in hem and [heading.]

French Pleats — This is a three-fold pleat and the [one most] often used in draperies.

H

Heading — The hemmed, usually stiffened, portic[n across] the top of a curtain or drapery.

Hem — Refers to finished sides and bottom ed[ges of] drapery.

Holdback — A decorative piece of hardware th[at holds] draperies to each side of the window.

I

Insert Pulley — An auxiliary traverse rod part, ov[er which] the cords operate.

J

Jabot — A decorative vertical end of an over treat[ment,] usually finishes a horizontal festoon.

Jamb — Interior sides of a door or window frame[.]

L

Lambrequin — A cornice that completely frames the [window.] Sometimes used interchangeably with val[ance or] cantonniere.

Laminated Weights — Weight covered on both side[s to prevent] rust marks on drapery.

Lanai — A type of window covering made up of a [series of] hinged, rigid plastic panels, hung from a traverse [rod.]

A fabric backing for a drapery.

Lintels are wood, steel, or reinforced concrete
ced over both window and door openings to hold
ll and roof above.

rrier — Two arms that overlap in center of rod
peries are closed, allowing draperies to close
y.

Trade name for a thermal lining.

Corner — The formation of the bottom edge of
ith a 45 degree angle on hem side.

The vertical wood or masonry sections between
f window frames.

v — A simultaneous opening and closing of several
on one rod at one time.

The horizontal wood strips that separate panes
windows.

r — A window not centered on a wall. Draperies
at its center point.

Draw — Drapery designed to draw one way only,
el.

f — This is on the back side of drapery and at top.
make one of the strongest type headings on any
his results when you carry both fabrics to the top
a turn with the crinoline.

- The overlap of a pair of draperies is that part of
panel which rides the master carrier of a traverse
verlaps in the center when draperies are drawn
ually 3½" on each side.

One half a pair of draperies or curtains.

epeat — The "repeat" of a pattern is the distance
ny given point in a design to where that exact point
d again.

ndow — A type of window with a large center glass
usually two smaller glass areas on each side.

ok — A metal pin to fasten draperies to a rod. It
rapery pleat and hooks to traverse carrier or cafe

ts — A drapery heading where the basic pleat is
two or three smaller, equal pleats, sewn together
om edge on the right side of the fabric.

fold of cloth sewn into place to create fullness.

- "Pleat To" is the finished width of the fabric after
pleated. Example: A width of 48" fabric has been
18" — "Pleat To" 18".

pe — Pocketed heading material designed to be
pleating hooks.

— Refers to a jutting out, an extension. On a
drapery rod, it is that part which returns to the wall
ont of the rod.

— A drapery tool by which exact angles are
(as in bay windows).

des — Standard size draperies, factory-made and
t local stores or through mail order sources.

The space from one design motif to the next one
rned fabric.

Return — The distance from the face of the rod to the wall
or casing where the bracket is attached.

Rod Pocket — A hollow sleeve in the top — and sometimes
the bottom — of a curtain or drapery through which a rod
is inserted. The rod is then attached to a solid wall surface.

S

Sash Curtain — Any sheer material hung close to the window
glass. Usually hung from spring tension rods or sash rods
mounted inside the window casing.

Sash Rod — A small rod, either decorative or plain, usually
mounted inside a window frame on the sash.

Scalloped Heading — A popular top treatment for cafe
curtains featuring semi-circular spaces between curtain rings.

Selvedge — The tightly woven edge on a width of fabric to
hold the fabric together.

Side Hem — The turned part forming a finished edge at the
side of the drapery.

Sill — The horizontal "ledge-like" portion of a window casing.

Slides — Small runners installed in a traverse rod which hold
a drapery pin or hook.

Spacing — Refers to the flat space between pleats; the fuller
the drapery, the less the spacing.

Stacking — The area required for draperies when they are
completely opened.

Swag — A section of draped fabric above a window.

T

Tension Pulley — The pulley attachment through which the
traverse cords move for one continuous smooth operation
when drapery is drawn. May be mounted on baseboard,
casing or wall, on one or both sides.

Tiebacks — Decorative pieces of hardware, sometimes
called holdbacks. Available in many forms and designed to
hold draperies back from the window to allow light passage
or add an additional decorative touch to the window
treatment.

Tier — Curtain layers arranged one above the other with a
normal overlap of 4". Upper tiers project from the wall at a
greater distance than lower panel to allow each curtain to
hang free.

Traverse — To draw across. A traverse drapery is one that
opens or closes across a window by means of the traverse
rod from which it is hung.

U

Under-Draperies — A lightweight drapery, usually a sheer,
closest to the window glass. It hangs beneath a heavier over-
drapery.

V

Valance — A valance is a horizontal decorative fabric
treatment used at the top of draperies to screen hardware
and cords.

W

Weights — (chain and lead) Lead weights are sewn
in at the vertical seams and each corner of drapery
panel. Chain weights are small beads strung in a line
along bottom hemline of sheers, to insure an even
hemline and straight hanging.

Width — A word to describe a single width of fabric.
Several widths of fabric are sewn together to make a
panel of drapery. "Panel" is sometimes used in
referring to a width of fabric.

Glossary of Fabrics and Fabric Terr

A

Antique Satin — One of the most common drapery fabrics sold. Characterized by a lustrous effect, normally composed of rayon/acetate blends.

B

Basketweave — Plain under-and-over weave; primarily in draperies.

Batiste — A soft finished fabric which has a high count of fine yarns. It is more opaque than voiles. Usually composed of 100% polyester or a polyester blend.

"Beta" Fiberglas Fiber — This filament is around .00010 inch in diameter, about one half the diameter of other glass fibers in use at present. Properties include improved flexibility, greater resistance to mechanical abuse to afford greater wearability, increased softness and suppleness and less irritation. "Beta" is used in apparel, home furnishings, and industrial fields. A registered trademark name of Owens-Corning Fiberglas Corp., N.Y.C.

Boucle — French for curled, indicates a curled or looped surface.

Brocade — Rich jacquard — woven fabric with all-over interwoven design of raised figures or flowers. Brocade has a raised surface in contrast to felt damask, and is generally made of silk, rayon and nylon yarns with or without metallic treatment.

Burlap — Coarse, canvas-like fabric made of jute, hemp or cotton. Also called Gunny.

C

Casements — Open weave casual fabric, characterized by its instability.

Challis — One of the softest fabrics made. Normally made of rayon and also combined with cotton.

Chintz — Glazed cotton fabric often printed with gay figures and large flower designs. Some glazes will wash out in laundering. The only durable glaze is a resin finish which will withstand washing or dry cleaning. Unglazed chintz is called cretonne.

Corduroy — A cut filling-pile cloth with narrow to wide wales which run in the warp direction of the goods and made possible by the use of an extra set of filling yarns in the construction. The back is of plain or twill weave, the latter affording the better construction. Washable types are available and stretch and durable press garments of corduroy are very popular. Usually an all-cotton cloth, some of the goods are now made with nylon or rayon pile effect on a cotton backing fabric or with polyester-cotton blends.

Crash — A coarse fabric having a rough irregular surface obtained by weavig thick uneven yarns. Usually cotton or linen, sometimes spun rayon or blends.

Crinoline — A heavily sized, stiff fabric used as a foundation to support the edge of a hem or puffed sleeve. Also used as interlining.

D

Damask — Firm, glossy jacquard-patterned fabric. Damask is similar to brocade, but flatter and reversible. It can be made from linen, cotton, rayon or silk, or a combination of fibers.

Double Knit — A fabric knitted with a double stitch on a double needle frame to provide a double thickness and is the same on both sides. It has excellent body and stability.

F

Faille — Plain weave (flat-rib); with filling yarns heavier than warp.

Foamback — Term used to denote that a fabric laminated to a backing of polyurethane foam.

G

Glasing — Thin finish provides luster, sheen, shine to some fabrics. Chintz is an example of a glaze

H

Hand, Handle — The reaction of the sense of tou fabrics are held in the hand. There are many fact give "character or individuality" to a material through handling. A correct judgement may thus concerning its capabilities in content, working pr drapability, feel, elasticity, fineness and s launderability, etc.

I

Inherent Flame Frees — Fabric woven of flame fabric (not processed) and flame-free for life of th

L

Linen — This is a product of the flax plant. An properties of linen are rapid moisture absorp fuzziness, does not soil quickly, a natural luster and

M

Matelasse — Appearance of a quilted weave; figure with a raised, bubbly surface.

Modacrylic — A modified fiber in which the fibe substance of any longchain synthetic polymer is c of less than 85%, but at least 25% of weight of ac units.

Mohair — Comes from the Angora goat, one of tl animals known to man. It is lighter weight drape slightly brushed or hairy finish.

Moire — A finish given cotton, silk, acetate, rayon, n where bright and dim effects are observed. This is by passing the fabric between engraved rollers wh the particular motif into the fabric.

N

Ninon — A smooth, transparent, high textured typ fabric. Usually made from 100% polyester.

O

Ombre — A graduate or shade effect of color used ir motif. Usually ranges from light to dark tones.

Organdy — Very light and thin, transparent, stiff cotton cloth. Will withstand repeated launderings a tain its crispness. Organdy is a true, durable finis

Satin Weave — One of the three basic weaves, t being plain weave and the twill weave. The surfac weave cloth is almost made up entirely of warp or fil since in the repeat of the weave, each yarn of the o passes or floats over or under all but one yarn of the yarn system. Satin weaves have a host of uses — brocatelle, damask other decorative materials.

Selvage — Each side edge of a woven fabric and part of the warp in the goods. Other names for it a self-edge, and raw edge.

Silk — The only natural fiber that comes in a filam reeled from the cocoon, cultivated or wild.

Slub Yarn — Yarn of any type which is irregular in may be caused by error, or purposely made with slub out some desired effect to enhance a material.

T

Taffeta — A fine plain weave fabric smooth on bo usually with a sheen on its surface.

y Cloth — This cloth fabric has uncut loops on both sides e cloth. Terry is also made on a Jacquard loom to form esting motifs.

ture — The first meaning is the actual number of warp ads and filling picks per inch in any cloth that has been en. Texture is also much used by the public and in rtising circles to mean the finish and appearance of cloth.

ad Count — 1. The actual number of warp ends and g picks per inch in a woven cloth. Texture is another name his term. 2. In knitted fabric, thread count implies the ber of wales or ribs, and the courses per inch.

ur — 1. A term loosely applied to cut pile cloths in eral; also to fabrics with a fine raised finish. 2. A cut pile n fabric comparable with cotton velvet, but with a greater

and denser pile. 3. A staple, high grade woolen fabric which has a close, fine, dense, erect, and even nap which provides a soft, pleasing hand.

Velvet — A warp pile cloth in which a succession of rows of short cut pile stand so close together as to give an even, uniform surface. When the pile is more than one-eighth of an inch high, the cloth is usually called plus.

Voile — A thin open mesh cloth made by a variation of plain weave. Most voiles are made of polyester. Similar to ninon, but with a much finer denier of yarn with a very soft, drapable hand.

W

Warp — The yarns which run vertically or lengthwise in woven fabric.

Weft Yarn — The yarn runs horizontal or cross yarns.

Drapery Fabrics — Look & Performance

Satins and Jacquards
Usually the most formal and traditional, they are generally made from tightly woven, heavy, soft material which hangs straight from top to bottom in (formal) folds.

Casements, Open Weaves
These have a lighter, more casual feel. They are usually made from loosely woven, textured yarns that hang in looser folds than the formal satins and Jacquards.

Sheers
Made of soft, see-through fabrics, sheers are appropriate in most decors. Light and airy, they are sometimes used in combination with heavier draperies in more formal settings. They are billowy unless weighted, and can be made to drape quite well.

Prints
Suitable in most decors, prints are made from a light, tightly woven fabric, usually cotton or cotton-polyester blends.

Drapery Linings
Linings add substantially to the luxurious appearance necessary for good window treatments, and also provide a fuller pleated look for maintaining a soft drapable hand.

The lined-look provides uniformity to the exterior appearance of a home while allowing a broad choice of textures, weaves, colors and patterns for the interior.

The combination of sunlight and air pollution will eventually take its toll on all colors. There is no such thing as an absolutely colorfast material or dye. Some colors, however will show fading more dramatically than others. Bright colors tend to show fading more than subdued tones, and solids before prints.

Linings help draperies last longer. They afford some protection against sun and fading. They also protect the draperies from water stains — either from condensation on the inside of the window or from a sudden shower.

Insulated linings contribute to energy conservation, keeping homes cooler in summer and warmer in winter.

Textile Fibers & Their Properties

NATURAL FIBERS

COTTON

Drapability:	excellent hang, soft hand
Color fastness:	good, vat dyes best
Sun resistance:	excellent, does not sun rot
Abrasion resistance:	excellent
Sagging:	does not stretch, except when wet
Resiliency:	poor, packs easily, wrinkles easily, very absorbent, burns
Care:	wash or dry clean and iron at high temperature

Cotton generally wears excellently in drapery (print or plains).

LINEN OR FLAX

Drapability:	good hang, but not as soft as cotton
Color fastness:	good to poor, prints do not hold their color as well as plain fabrics
Sun resistance:	excellent, does not sun rot
Abrasion resistance:	excellent
Sagging:	strong, does not stretch
Resiliency:	poor, packs badly, does wrinkle
Care:	dry clean and iron at high temperature

Linens are excellent in plain and casement fabric and good in prints.

SILK

Drapability:	good hang, medium to soft hand
Color fastness:	good
Sun resistance:	poor, rots in short time, lining helps
Abrasion resistance:	good
Sagging:	strong, does not sag
Resiliency:	good, does not pack badly
Care:	dry clean and iron at medium temperature

Little silk is used in drapery today. This is due to sun rot and cost.

WOOL

There is virtually none used in drapery fabric.

MAN-MADE

RAYON

Drapability:	good hang, soft hand
Color fastness:	good to excellent (solution dyed)
Sun resistance:	good, but not as good as cotton or linen
Abrasion resistance:	good, but not as good as nylon or cotton
Sagging:	poor, stretches in loose yarns, but OK in tight woven fabrics
Resiliency:	good, does not pack, wrinkles less than cotton or linen
Care:	dry clean and iron at medium temperature

Rayon is blended with other fibers: cotton, acetate and linen.

ACETATE

Drapability:	good hand, soft hand
Color fastness:	good (solution dyed)
Sun resistance:	good, not as good as cotton and linen
Abrasion resistance:	good, but not as good as cotton or nylon
Sagging:	poor stretches in loose yarns, but OK in tight woven fabrics
Resiliency:	good, does not pack, wrinkles less than cotton or linen
Care:	dry clean and iron at low temperature

Blends well with other fibers, rayon and nylon.

POLYESTER

Drapability:	excellent hang, very soft hand
Color fastness:	good to excellent
Sun resistance:	excellent
Abrasion resistance:	good, sheers must be handled with care. Fabric can be bruised.
Sagging:	excellent, does not stretch or shrink
Resiliency:	good to excellent, does not pack, wrinkle free
Care:	wash or dry clean and iron at low temp temperature

Polyester is an excellent fabric for most drapery applications. It blends well with other fibers. In polyester cotton blends, cotton wrinkles less.

NYLON

Drapability:	good, soft to stiff hand, not as soft as polyesters
Color fastness:	good to excellent
Sun resistance:	poor
Abrasion resistance:	excellent
Sagging:	excellent, does not sag
Resiliency:	excellent, does not pack, wrinkle free
Care:	dry clean and iron at low temperature

Nylon is not widely used in drapery fabric.

ACRYLIC

Drapability:	excellent, very soft hand
Color fastness:	excellent, if solution dyed
Sun resistance:	excellent, good as cotton or linen
Abrasion resistance:	good
Sagging:	very good, does not stretch
Resiliency:	very good, does not pack and wrinkle
Care:	dry clean and iron at low temperature

Acrylic fabrics hang well and do not sag. Can be blended with polyester. Modacrylics are flameproof.

DYNEL

Drapability:	excellent, soft hand like acrylic
Color fastness:	excellent
Sun resistance:	good to excellent
Abrasion resistance:	excellent
Sagging:	excellent compared to rayon or acetate
Resiliency:	very good, does not pack, wrinkle free low flamability
Care:	Wash only, ironing does not affect it much, use low heat

WINDOWS WITH A CHALLENGE

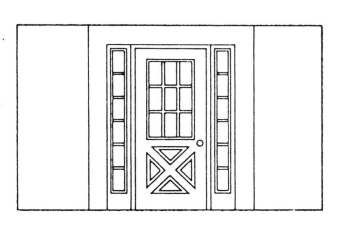

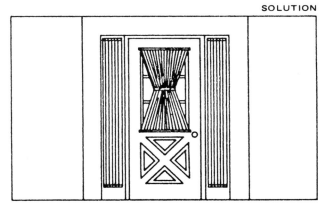

SOLUTION

Door With Window & Sidelights

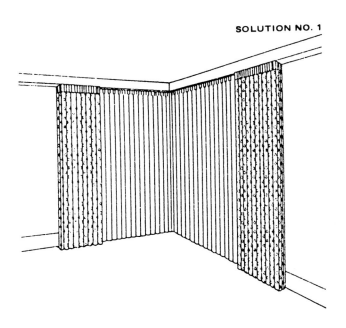

SOLUTION NO. 1

Corner Gliding Windows With Structural Beam Atop

SOLUTION NO. 2

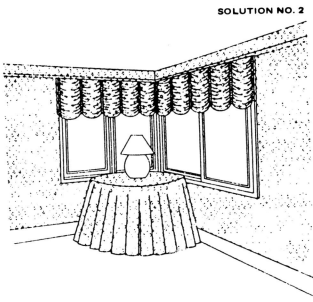

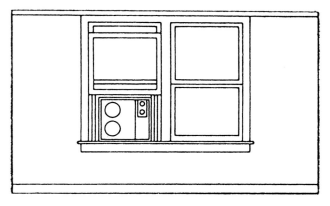

Air Conditioner in a Double Hung Window

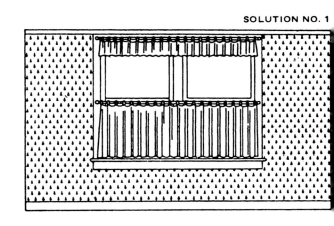

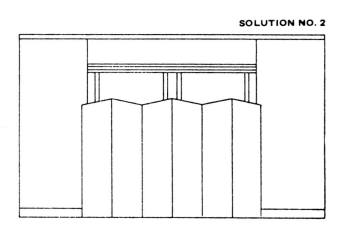

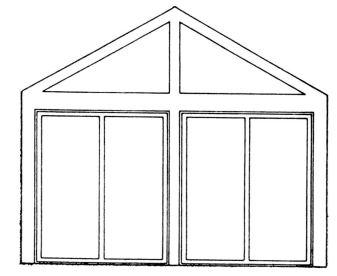

Sliding Glass Doors & Cathedral Windows

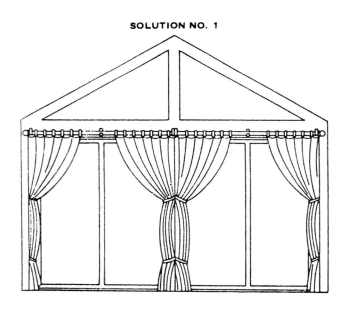

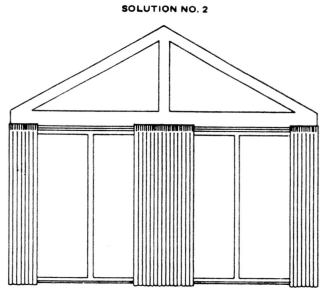

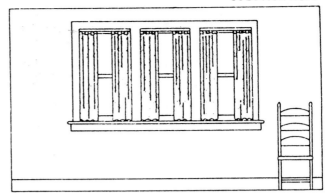
SOLUTION NO. 1

Triple Double-Hung Window

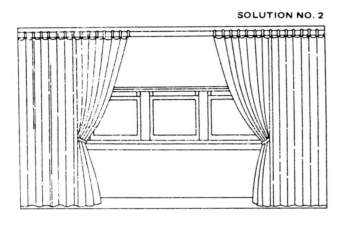
SOLUTION NO. 2

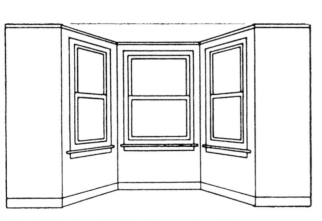

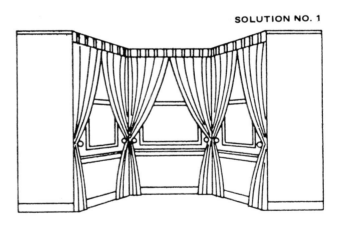
SOLUTION NO. 1

Bay Window With Casement Windows

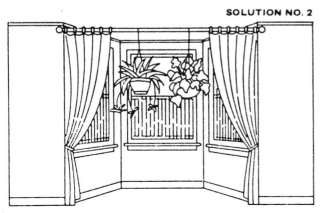
SOLUTION NO. 2

SOLUTION NO. 3

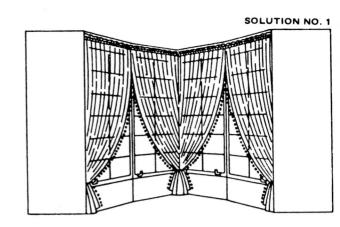

Bay Window With Casement Windows

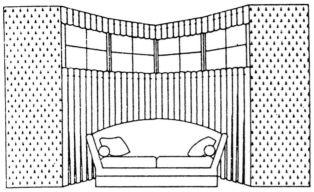

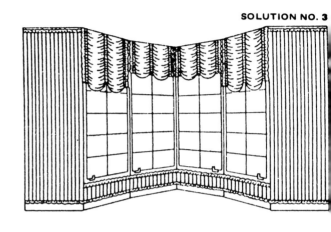

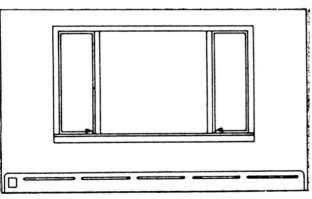

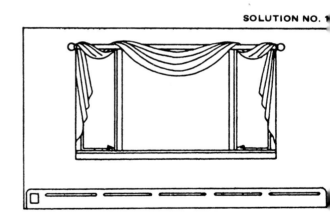

Picture Window With Baseboard Radiator

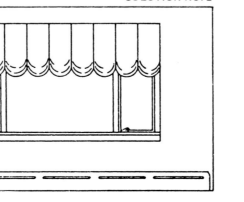

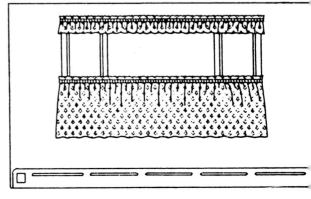

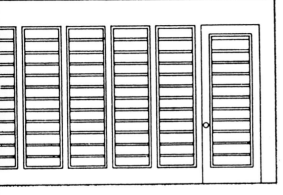

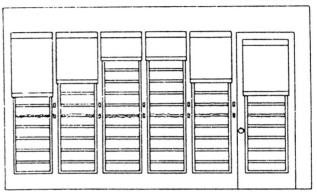

usie Windows & Door

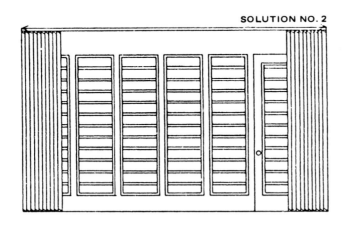

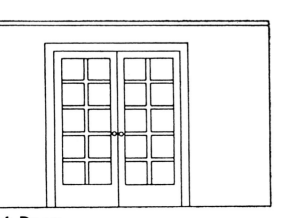

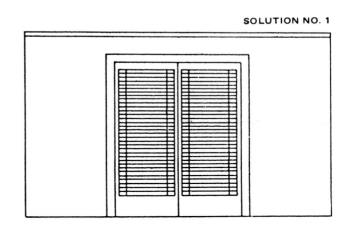

nch Doors

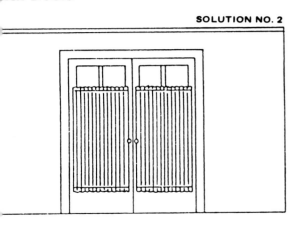

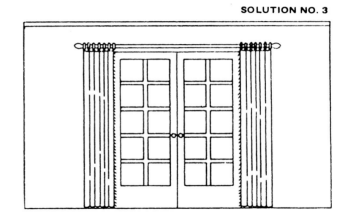

Fan Windows

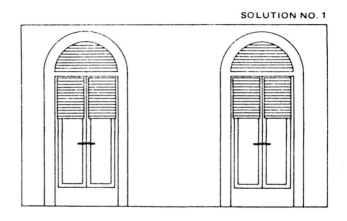

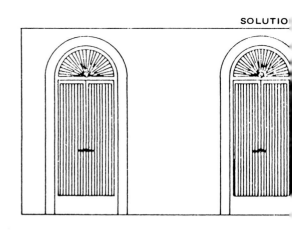

Basic Window Types

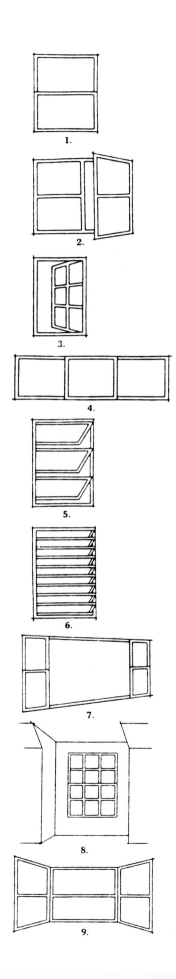

Double Hung Window — Most common of all window types, has two sashes, one or both of which slide up and down. Unless it is too long and narrow or in the wrong location, this type of window is usually one of the easiest to decorate.

In-Swinging Casement — Opens into the room. If it is not decorated properly, curtains and draperies may tangle with the window as it is opened and closed.

Out-Swinging Casement — Opens outward. Both in-swinging and out-swinging casements may be operated by a crank, or simply moved by hand. Out-swinging casements are easily decorated.

Ranch or Strip Windows — Most often a wide window set high off the floor. Usually has sliding sashes and is common to most ranch type houses. It requires special consideration when decorating to make it attractive.

Awning Window — Has wide, horizontal sashes that open outward to any angle; can usually be left open when it's raining. Unless it is awkwardly placed or shaped, it's an easy one to decorate.

Jalousie Window — Identified by narrow, horizontal strips of glass that open by means of a crank to any desired angle. Decorating problems result only when the shape or location is unusual.

Picture Window — One designed to frame an outside view. It may consist of one large, fixed pane of glass, in which case the window cannot be opened. Or it may have movable sections on one or both sides of a fixed pane — or above and below — which can be opened for ventilation. Sometimes there are decorating problems, but in general, a picture window is your big opportunity.

Dormer Window — Usually a small window projecting from the house in an alcove-like extension of the room. It requires a treatment all its own.

Bay Windows — Three or more windows set at an angle to each other in a recessed area. You can use lots of imagination with bay windows.

10. **Bow Window** — A curved window, sometimes called a circular bay.

11. **Slanting Window** — Often called "cathedral" window, usually an entire wall of the room. Its main characteristic is the angle at the top where the window follows the line of a slanting roof. This top slanting line often causes decorating concern, but the problem can be solved very effectively.

12. **Double Windows** — Side by side windows. (If there are more than one they are often called multiple windows.) Most often treated as a single unit, always think of them together, as one decorating element.

13. **Corner Windows** — Any window that comes together at the corner of a room.

14. **French Doors** — Sometimes called French windows. They come in pairs and often open onto a porch or patio. Usually they need special decorating to look their best.

15. **Sliding Glass Doors** — Today's functional version of French doors. They are often set into a regular wall, but are sometimes part of a modern "glass wall." Either way, they need special decor that allows them to serve as doors yet provide nighttime privacy.

16. **Clerestory Window** — A shallow window set near the ceiling. Usually should be decorated inconspicuously. (In modern architecture, it is sometimes placed in the slope of a beamed ceiling, in which case it should rarely be decorated at all.)

17. **Palladian Window** — An arched top window with straight panes below the arch.

18 **Glass Wall** — Usually a group of basic window units made to fit together, forming a veritable "wall" of windows. Curtains and draperies often require special planning.

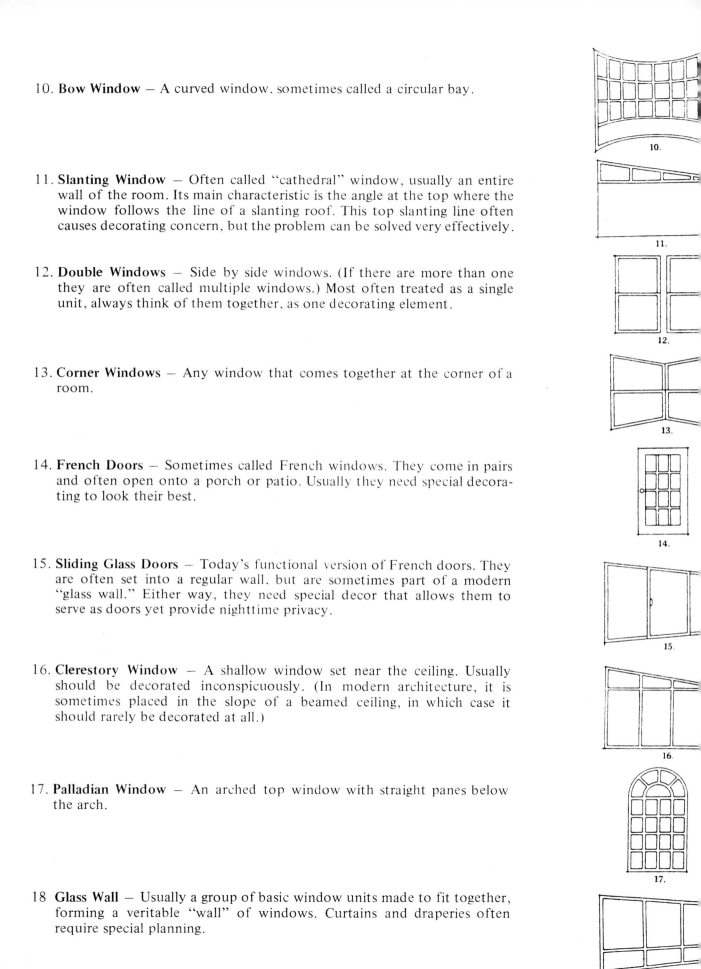

Stationary Draperies gathered on rod
Curved Sleeve-Valance with Bows

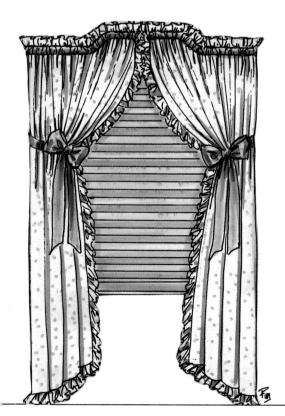

Ruffled Tied-back Drapery
gathered on Arched Rod -
Duette Shade under

Double Continental
with high Bow Tie-Backs-
Wood Blind under

Arched Rod with Stand-Up Ruffle
& Bishop Sleeve Draperies

Austrian Valance with Ruffled over
Ruffled Cafe Curtain

Double Rod Valance with
Ruffled Tied-back Draperies

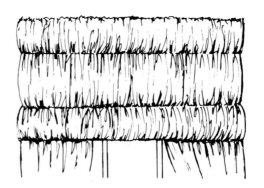

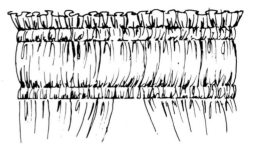

Alternate Heading Styles

Continental
eading

cket Side Treatment
od Sleeve

Bishop Sleeve Draperies with Valance

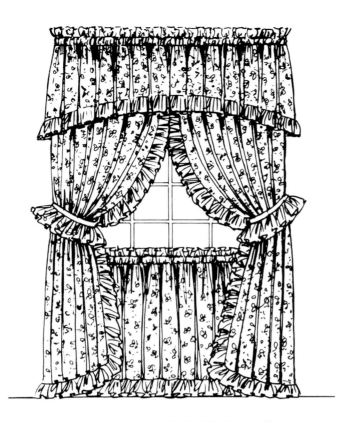

Arched Valance with Ruffle & Ruffled
Tie-backs over Cafe Curtains

Tie-back Draperies with Balloon Val

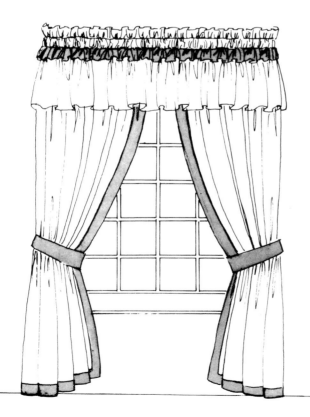

Tied-back Draperies with Accent Band –
Shirred Valance

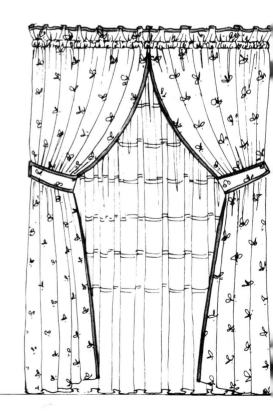

Tie-backs with Ruffle at top –
Sheers under

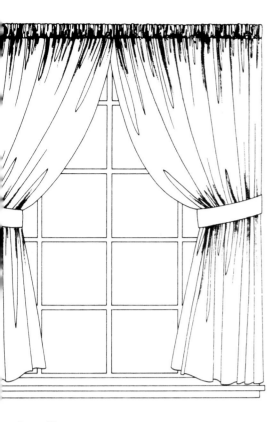

ocket Drapery

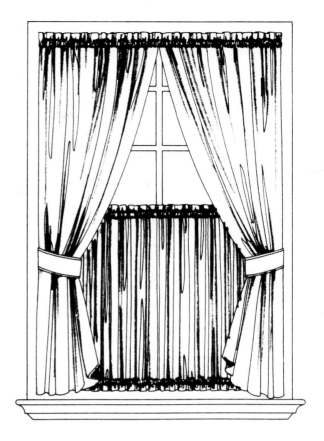

The Layered Look

ng And Casing Top Only

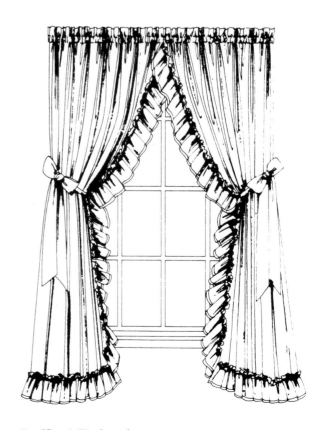

Ruffled Tieback

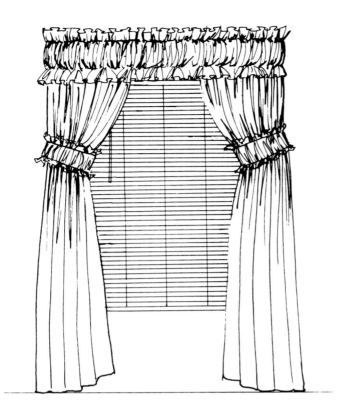

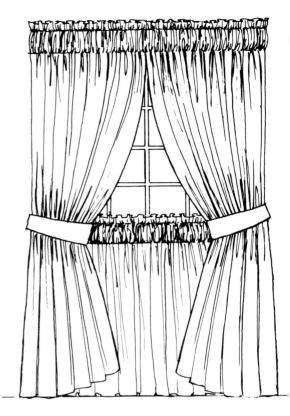

Rod Top & Bottom Valance with matching
Shirred Tie-bands – Mini Blind

Tied-back Draperies with Continental
Matching Cafe Curtain under

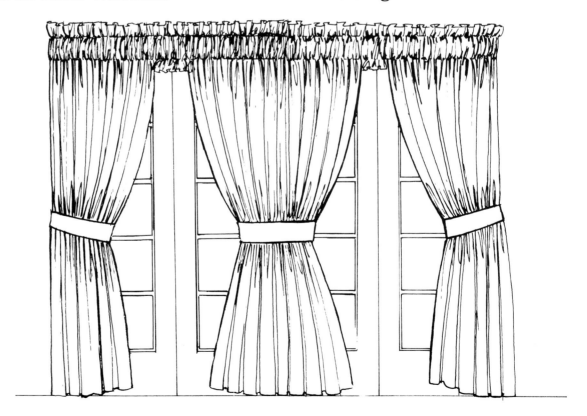

Triple Tie-backs on Continental Rod with Stand-up Top

ck Stationary Draperies on Dec. Pole
eve in middle

Rod Top Draperies on Dec Pole

d Bishop Sleeve Draperies
d on Dec Rod

Stationary Rod Top Draperies on Dec
Pole – Sleeve in middle

Kingston Valance over Tied-back
Draperies – Sheers under

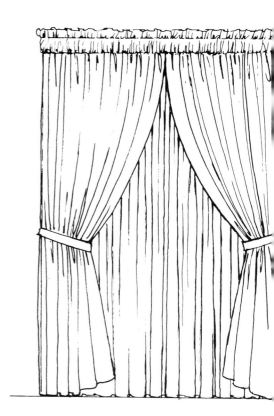

Continental Rod with Tie-backs
over sheers

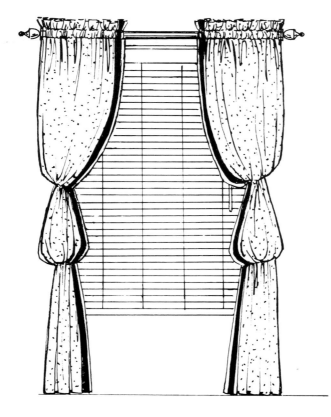

Banded Stationary Bishop's Sleeve
over Mini Blind

Stationary Drapery on Covered R
with 3″ Stand-up Top

Cluster Pleated Valance on Dec Rod with
pleated Draperies over Roman Shade

ench Pleated Draperies on Dec. Rod
ver Balloon Shade

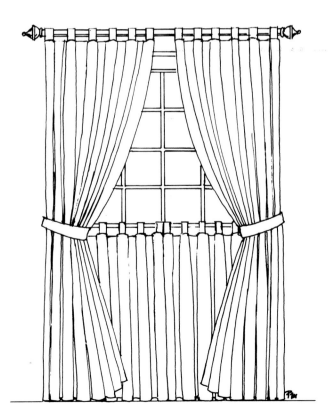

Tab Draperies on Dec. Rod over Cafe
Curtain

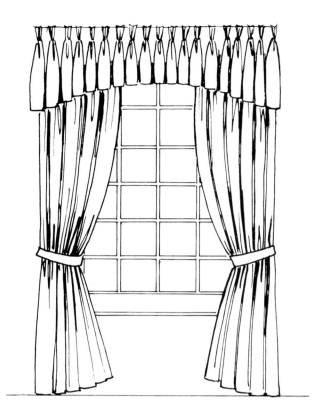

Arched French Pleated Valance
& Tie-backs

Multiple Arched Valance over Dra
& Sheers

Cloud Valance on Continental Rod
Tie-back Draperies over Sheers

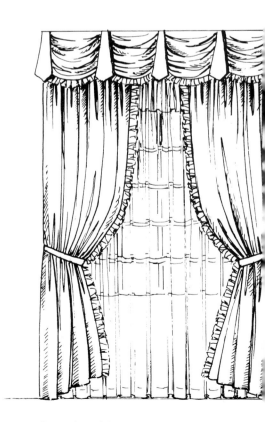

Austrian Valance with Tie-backs
over Sheers

Rod Top Draperies with Center Florence
& low Tie-backs over Mini Blind

Draperies gathered on Dec. Pole
over Austrian Shade

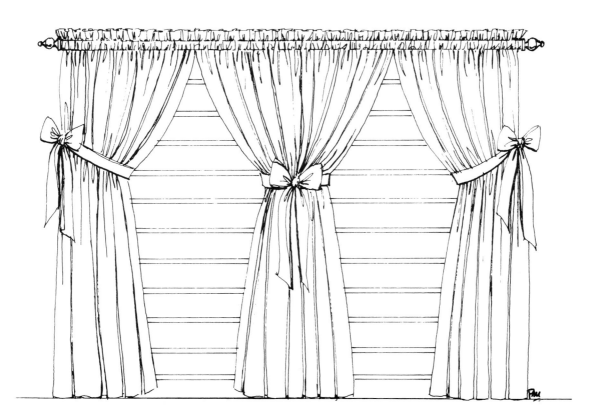

Rod Top Draperies with Multiple Bow Ties over Roman Shade

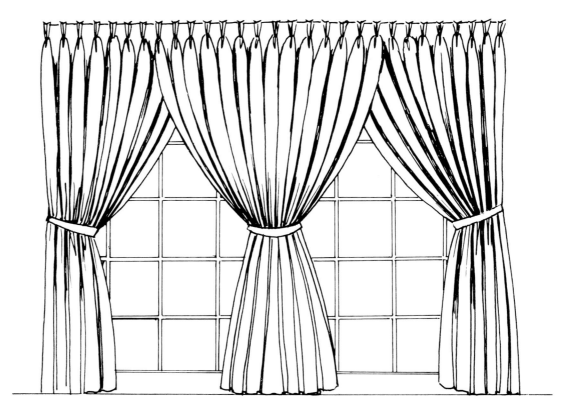

Multiple Tie Back Draperies

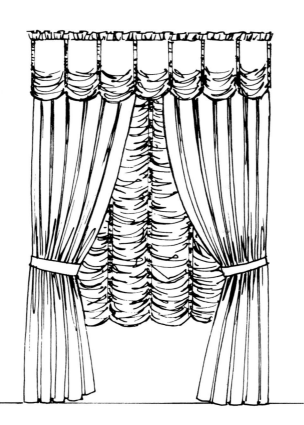

Tie-back Draperies with Austrian
Valance & Shade

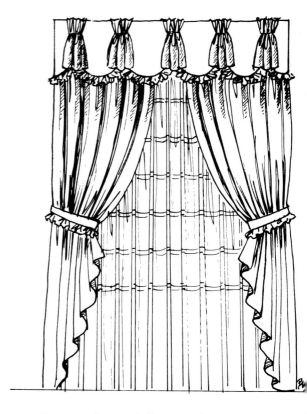

Space pleated Queen Ann Valance wi
scalloped edge over Tie-backs & She

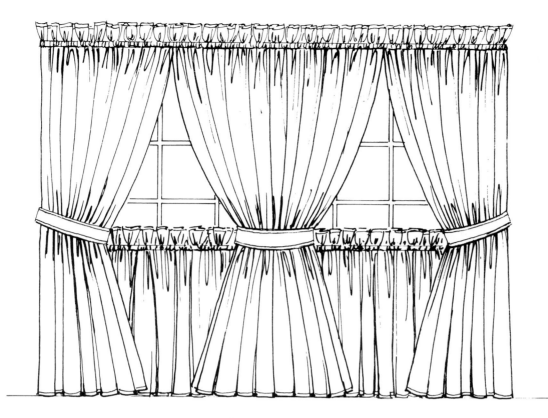

Multiple Tie-backs over Cafe Curtains for a warm Country feeling

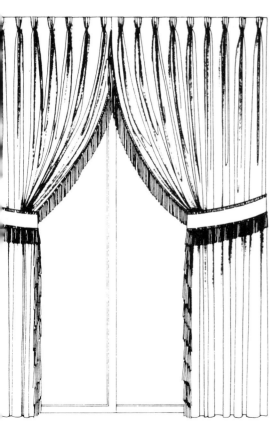

Pinch-Pleated Drapery
With Fringe

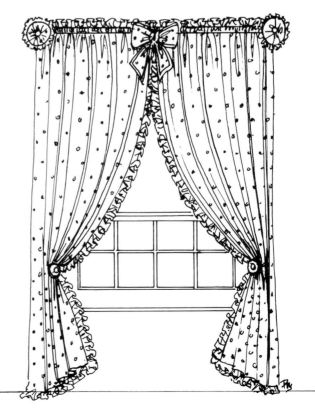

Ruffled Tie-backs with Bow & Rosettes
over Pull-down Shade

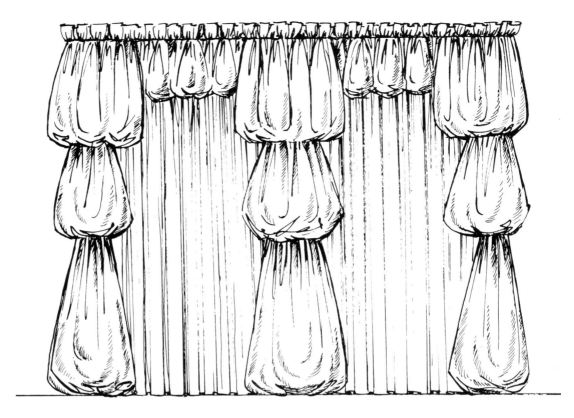

Rod Top Only Balloon Draperies

Double Rod Top Valance with
Puffed Tie-backs over Sheers

End-pleated Valance with Puffed
Tie-backs over Lace Curtain

ustom Made Draperies

ndard Workmanship and
lity Features

uble Heading
'ermanent Buckram Headings
ating custom tacked with extra thread
seams serged and overlocked
draperies perfectly matched
draperies table sized
d stitched bottom and side hems
uble 4″ bottom hems + 1½″ Double side hems
draperies weighted at corners and seams.
ltiple width draperies are pleated so that joining seams
hidden behind pleats.

ade to Custom Measurements

any exact width or length.
ated to any desired fullness up to 3 to 1.
ed or unlined.

apery Terminology

dth is one strip of material (can be any length) which can
pleated to a finished dimension across the TOP of between
and 24″. Using a 48″ wide material as our base, a width of
ch finishes to 24″ is considered double fullness or 2 to 1;
finished width is considered triple fullness or 3 to 1. Any
nber of widths can be joined together to make the
peries properly cover the window area.
el is a single unit of drapery of one or more widths, which
sed specifically for one way draw — stack left or stack
t — and/or stationary units.
r is two equal panels which are pleated to cover a desired
a.
urn is the measurement from the rod to the wall; in other
rds the projection.
erlap is the measurement, when draperies are fully closed,
aving the right panel overlap the left panel. This is usually
or each panel. *Remember your customer must add 12″ to*
rod measurement to insure proper returns and overlaps.

ions Available on Draperies

iety of Headings:
ch Pleated with 4″ buckram
ch Pleated with 5″ buckram
 Pleated
 Pleated with Tabs for rod. Add diameter of rod to
inished length. For flat tab draperies use 2-1.
d Pocket for shirred draperies.
peries may be self-lined, or
peries may be lined with black-out lining.

Pleat Spacing

Pleat spacings vary according to the widths of material used to achieve a specified finished width. For example: 3 widths of material pleated to 59 inches to the pair will not have the same pleat spacing as 3 widths of material pleated to 72 inches to the pair. If pleats and pleat spacing are to look alike on draperies of different widths, please specify "comparable fullness" on your order. *Vertically striped fabrics will not fabricate to allow an identical stripe to fall between each pleat, panel to panel, or pair to pair.*

How to Order Your Draperies

Since "Made-to-Measure" draperies are made to your exact specifications it is imperative that measurements be made with the greatest of care. We recommend that you double check all measurements for accuracy. All measuring should be done with a steel tape or yardstick. Measure each window separately even when they appear to be the same size. If length varies use dimension of shortest length.

Drapery Width

- Measure width of drapery rod from end to end.
- Add to this figure an extra 12″ to include the allowance for standard traverse rod returns and overlap.
- Standard returns are 3″ in depth. For over-draperies allow for clearance of under-curtain. A 6″ return should be sufficient.
- When ordering panels that stack (draw) in one direction only, specify if the drapery is to stack (draw) left or right.

Drapery Length

- Measure from top of rod, to floor or to carpet. (By inserting pins 1″ from top drapery will automatically clear the floor or carpet.)
- Under-curtain should be at least ½″ shorter than over-drapery.
- When floor length draperies are used it is best to measure length at each side and in the center. Use shortest figure for your measurement.
- Rod should be placed a minimum of 4″ above the window so hooks and pleats will not be observed from outside.
- If sill length, allow 4″ below sill so bottom hem will not be observed from outside.
- When using pole rings, measure length from bottom of rings.

Caution: When both under-curtain and over-drapery are used, be sure to allow for clearance of face drapery. For example, an under-curtain with a 3½″ return requires at least a 6″ return on the over-drapery.

YARDAGE CHART FOR 4'' OR 5'' HEADING (Cut Plus 20'')

TOTAL NUMBER OF WIDTHS PER PAIR OR PANEL

FINISHED LENGTH	2W	3W	4W	5W	6W	7W	8W	9W	10W	11W	12W	13W	14W	15W
36″	3¼	4¾	6¼	7¾	9¼	10¾	12¼	13¾	15¼	16¾	18¼	19¾	21¼	22¾
40″	3½	5	6½	8	9½	11	12½	14	15½	17	18½	20	21½	23
44″	3¾	5½	7¼	9	10¾	12½	14¼	16	17¾	19½	21¼	23	24¾	26½
48″	4	5¾	7½	9¼	11	12¾	14½	16¼	18	19¾	21½	23¼	25	26¾
52″	4	6	8	10	12	14	16	18	20	22	24	26	28	30
56″	4¼	6½	8½	10¾	12¾	15	16¾	19	21¼	23¼	25½	27½	29¾	31¾
60″	4½	6¾	9	11¼	13½	15¾	18	20	22¼	24½	26¾	29	31¼	33½
64″	4¾	7	9½	11¾	14	16½	18¾	21	23½	25¾	28	30½	32¾	35
68″	5	7½	10	12¼	14¾	17¼	19¾	22	24½	27	29½	32	34¼	36¾
72″	5¼	7¾	10¼	13	15½	18	20½	23	25¾	28¼	30¾	33¼	36	38½
76″	5½	8	10¾	13½	16	18¾	21½	24	26¾	29½	32	34¾	37½	40
80″	5¾	8½	11¼	14	16¾	19½	22¼	25	28	30¾	33½	36¼	39	41¾
84″	6	8¾	11¾	14½	17½	20¼	23¼	26	29	32	34¾	37¾	40½	43½
88″	6	9	12	15	18	21	24	27	30	33	36	39	42	45
92″	6¼	9½	12½	15¾	18¾	22	25	28	31¼	34¼	37½	40½	43¾	46¾
96″	6½	9¾	13	16¼	19½	22¾	26	29	32¼	35½	38¾	42	45¼	48½
100″	6¾	10	13½	16¾	20	23½	26¾	30	33½	36¾	40	43½	46¾	50
104″	7	10½	14	17¼	20¾	24¼	27¾	31	34½	38	41½	45	48¼	51¾
108″	7¼	10¾	14¼	18	21½	25	28½	32	35¾	39¼	42¾	46¼	50	53½

STACK BACK CHART

THE GLASS IS	TOTAL STACK-BACK SHOULD BE	ROD LENGTH AND DRAPERY COVERAGE SHOULD BE
38 inches	26 inches	64 inches
44	28	72
50	30	80
56	32	88
62	34	96
68	36	104
75	37	112
81	39	120
87	41	128
94	42	136
100	44	144
106	46	152
112	48	160
119	49	168
125	51	176
131	53	184
137	55	192
144	56	200
150	58	208
156	60	216
162	62	224
169	63	232
175	65	240
181	67	248
187	69	255

ou will have to ADD RETURNS AND OVERLAPS TO DRAPERY COVERAGE.

ART IS BASED ON AVERAGE PLEATING AND MEDIUM WEIGHT FABRIC. YOU MAY DEDUCT
ᴹ ROD LENGTH IF YOU ARE USING A ONE WAY ROD. IF BULKY FABRIC IS USED, ADD TO
ACK ACCORDINGLY.

PLEAT-TO / FULLNESS CHARTS

(48" Fabric) 2½ X's Fullness

PLEAT-TO	19	38	57	76	95	114	133	152	171	190	209	228	247	266
WIDTHS	1	2	3	4	5	6	7	8	9	10	11	12	13	14

(48" Fabric) 3 X's Fullness

PLEAT-TO	15	30	45	60	75	90	105	120	135	150	165	180	195	210
WIDTHS	1	2	3	4	5	6	7	8	9	10	11	12	13	14

(54" Fabric) 2½ X's Fullness

PLEAT-TO	21	42	63	84	105	126	147	168	189	210	231	254	273	294
WIDTHS	1	2	3	4	5	6	7	8	9	10	11	12	13	14

(54" Fabric) 3 X's Fullness

PLEAT-TO	17	34	51	68	85	102	119	136	153	170	187	204	221	238
WIDTHS	1	2	3	4	5	6	7	8	9	10	11	12	13	14

FULLNESS CHART

48" Fabric	Pleated to 2½ X's fullness = 19" Panels
54" Fabric	Pleated to 2½ X's fullness = 21" Panels
60" Fabric	Pleated to 2½ X's fullness = 23" Panels

48" Fabric	Pleated to 3 X's fullness = 15" Panels
54" Fabric	Pleated to 3 X's fullness = 17" Panels
60" Fabric	Pleated to 3 X's fullness = 19" Panels

48" Fabric	Pleated to 2 X's fullness = 23" Panels
54" Fabric	Pleated to 2 X's fullness = 26" Panels
60" Fabric	Pleated to 2 X's fullness = 29" Panels

PLEAT TO CHART

Heavy Duty Rods

Oneway 3½" return add 5 inches
Center Open 3½ return add 12 inch

One Way 6" return add 7 inches
Center Open 6" return add 16 inch

Decorator Type Rods

One Way 3½" return add 7 inches
Center Open 3½" add 16 inches

One Way 6" return add 9 inches
Center Open 6" return add 19 inch

...hed Valance with Bows
...thered on Rod

Cloud Valance with Stand-up Ruffle

...ultiple Swagged Valance with Jabots

Plain Banded Valance with Jabots

...ab-top Valance on Dec. Rod

Multiple Arched Valance Shirred on Rod

Rolled Stagecoach Valance
with Wide Knotted Tie Bands

Swags & Jabots over Plain Valance

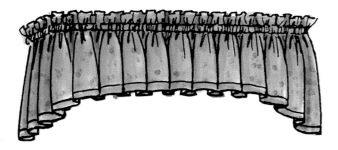

Arched Valance with Top Ruffle

Gathered Valance on Top & Bottom Rods
with Multiple Bow Ties

Double Pinch Pleat

V101

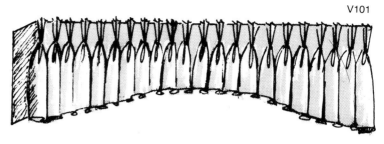

Pleated Arched Valance

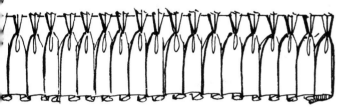

ch Pleated Valance

V103

Double Pleat Queen Ann

04

ce Pleated Valance

V105

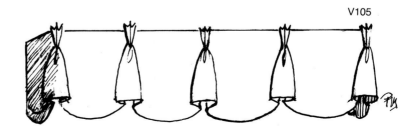

Queen Ann Valance

V137

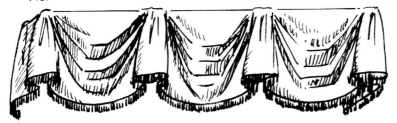

Kingston Valance

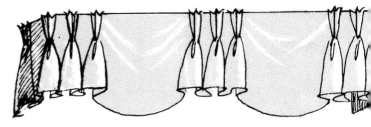

Space Pleated Queen Ann Valance

V108

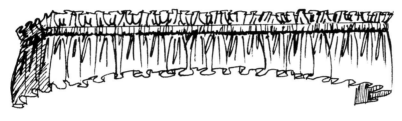

RTO Arched Valance

RTO Valance

V110

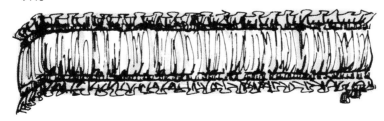

RTB Valance

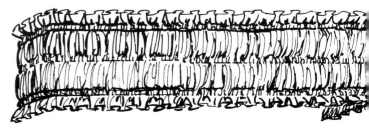

Double RTB Valance

12

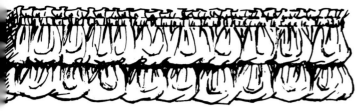

uble RTB Valance

V113

RTB Valance with Lower Rod Lifted

V114

oud Valance with Shirred Heading

V115

Cloud Valance with Continental Heading

16

Cloud Valance with Stand-up Ruffle

V117

Balloon Valance with Welting

V118

Rod Top Swag & Cascade

V119

RTO Tapered Valance

V120

RTO Swag & Jabot Valance

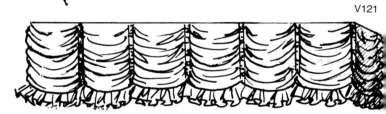

V121

Austrian with Ruffles

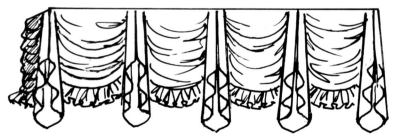

V122

Austrian with Jabots

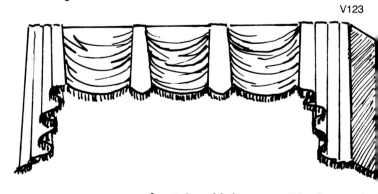

V123

Austrian Valance with Cascades

Roman with Ties

V124

Mock Roman

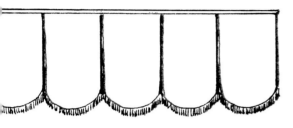

oped Valance with Fringed Edge

V126

Inverted Box Pleat

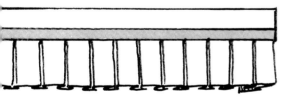

ed Box Pleat with Banding

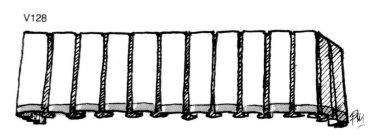

V128

Box Pleat with Banding

V130

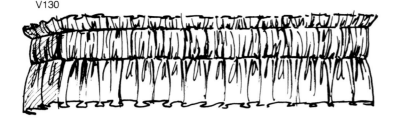

Continental with Standup Ruffle

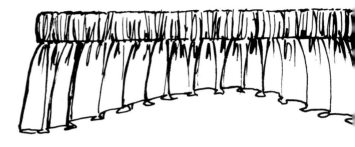

Arched Continental

V141

Double Continental with
Standup Top & Bottom

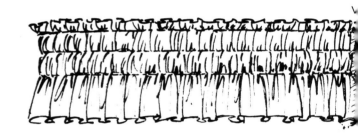

Double Continental with Stand

V142

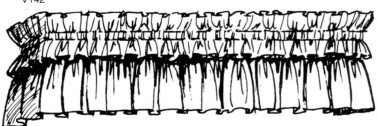

Double Ruffled Valance Shirred on Rod

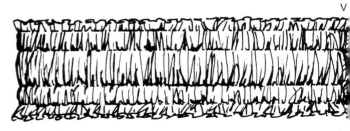

Continental RTB with Stand

ental Heading with No Standup

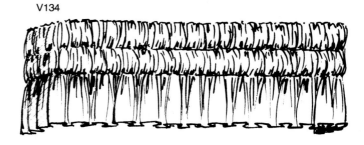

V134

Double Continental with No Standup

Continental Cloud Valance

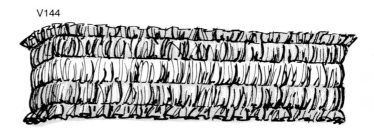

V144

Triple Continental with Multiple Fabrics

ed Heading

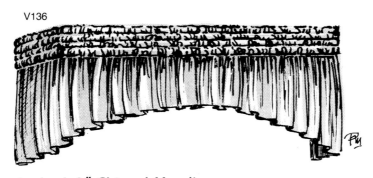

V136

Arched 4″ Shirred Heading

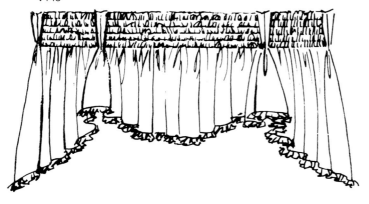

V145

Shirred Double Arched Valance with Spaced Pleats

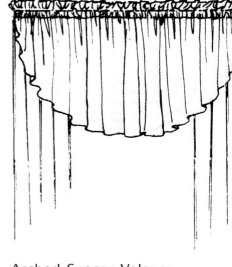

V146

Arched Spacer Valance

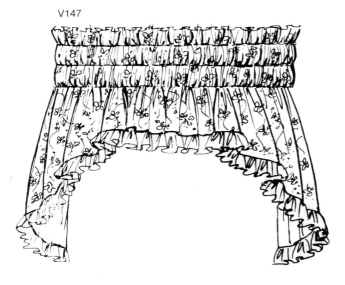

V147

Double Continental with Ruffles
& Tapered Sides

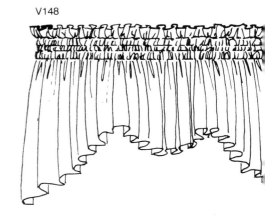

V148

Double Arched Valance with Shi
Heading & Tapered Sides

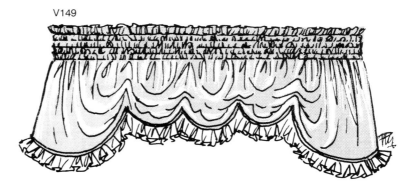

V149

Shirred Cloud Valance with Dropped Sides & Ruffle

CONTINENTAL™ is a registered trademark of Kirsch-Cooper Industries.

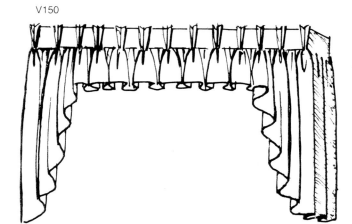

V150

French Pleated Valance

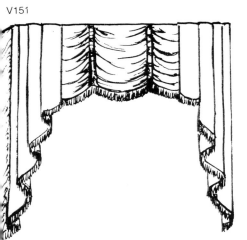

V151

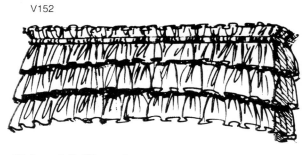

V152

Shirred 3-Tiered
Petticoat Valance

Austrian Valance With
Side Cascades

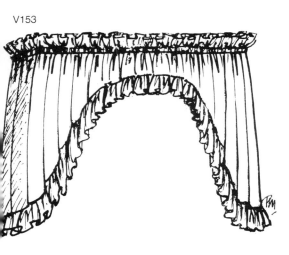

V153

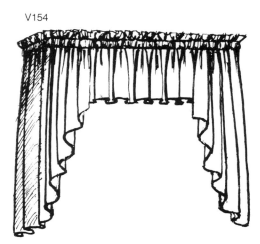

V154

New Orleans Valance
With 6" Ruffle

Rod Pocket Valance
With Tapered Sides

YARDAGE INFORMATION

GENERAL TERMS

PLEAT-TO: Rod or Board facing plus returns.

FINISHED LENGTH: Length after fabrication. That is, the length you want the valance to be after the wo[...] makes it.

CUT LENGTH: Is the length of material figured per width consisting of the finished length plus the n[...] of inches your workroom requires for heading, bottom hem, possible repeat, and allowance for trim[...]

WIDTHS: Each piece of drapery fabric sewn together to form a pair or panel of draperies is a width. Ex[...] a one way panel of draperies with a pleat-to of 110'' requires 6 widths of 48'' fabric. See fullness c[...]

FULLNESS: The more fabric you pleat-to, or gather together to fill a given space. Usually two, two and[...] or three times fullness.

REPEAT: How many inches a pattern takes to repeat itself.

PLEAT-TO / FULLNESS CHARTS

(48'' Fabric) 2½ X's Fullness

PLEAT-TO	19	38	57	76	95	114	133	152	171	190	209	228	247	266
WIDTHS	1	2	3	4	5	6	7	8	9	10	11	12	13	14

(48'' Fabric) 3 X's Fullness

PLEAT-TO	15	30	45	60	75	90	105	120	135	150	165	180	195	210
WIDTHS	1	2	3	4	5	6	7	8	9	10	11	12	13	14

(54'' Fabric) 2½ X's Fullness

PLEAT-TO	21	42	63	84	105	126	147	168	189	210	231	254	273	294
WIDTHS	1	2	3	4	5	6	7	8	9	10	11	12	13	14

(54'' Fabric) 3 X's Fullness

PLEAT-TO	17	34	51	68	85	102	119	136	153	170	187	204	221	238
WIDTHS	1	2	3	4	5	6	7	8	9	10	11	12	13	14

YARDAGE REQUIREMENTS

V100, V101, V102, V103, V104, V105, V106, V107, V108, V109, V129, V130, V133, V135, V136, V137,[...] V142, V143, V144, V145, V146, V148.

For these valances determine widths required and fullness using fullness charts above. Gathered style va[...] usually look better with 300 percent fullness.

SELF LINED PLAIN FABRIC (recommended fullness 2½ - 3 X's)

Double finished length plus 10'' equals cut length. Cut length X's widths required divided by 36 equals ya[...]

PLAIN FABRIC WITH LINING

Finished length plus 10'' X's required widths divided by 36 equals yardage. If you use lining for valance[...] V101, V103, V105, V106, and V107 the lining may show from certain angles. For this reason, I feel its b[...] self-line these valances.

d length plus 10'' divided by repeat, rounded to higher whole number (if number is fractional). Whole r X's repeat equals cut length. Cut length X's widths needed divided by 36 equals yardage. Its better lining for print. This is because the print may bleed through in the light if self-lined.

V111, V131, V134,

ine widths required using fullness charts. Gathered style valances usually look better with 300 percent s.

INED PLAIN FABRIC

finished length plus 14'' equals cut length. Cut length X's widths divided by 36 equals yardage.

FABRIC WITH LINING

d length plus 14'' equals cut lenght. Cut length X's widths divided by 36 equals yardage.

ED FABRICS WITH LINING (lining recommended)

d length plus 16'' divided by repeat, rounded to higher whole number (if number is fractional). Whole r X's repeat equals cut length. Cut length X's widths required divided by 36 equals yardage.

ine widths required using fullness charts. Gathered style valances usually look better with 300 percent s.

FABRIC UNLINED OR LINED (self-lined not recommended)

d length plus 32'' equals cut length. Widths required X's cut length divided by 36 equals yardage. The ength is needed because the installer lifts the lower rods to give the valance a cloud like look.

ED FABRICS WITH LINING (recommended)

d length plus 30'' divided by repeat, then rounded to higher whole number (if number is fractional). number X's repeat equals cut length. Cut length X's widths required divided by 36 equals yardage. tra length is needed because the installer lifts the lower rods to give the valance a cloud like look.

FABRIC UNLINED OR LINED

d length plus 24'' equals cut length. Widths required X's cut length divided by 36 equals yardage.

ED FABRICS WITH LINING (recommended)

d length plus 22'' divided by repeat, then rounded to higher whole number (if number is fractional). number X's repeat equals cut length. Cut length X's widths required divided by 36 equals yardage.

V116, V117.

FABRIC WITH LINING (lining recommended)

d length plus 20'' equals cut length. Pleat-to X's 3 divided by fabric width, then round to next whole This equals number of widths required. Widths required X's cut length divided by 36 equals yardage.

PRINTED FABRICS WITH LINING (recommended)

Finished length plus 20'' divided by repeat, then rounded to higher whole number (if number is fraction) Whole number X's repeat equals cut length. Pleat-to X's 3 divided by fabric width, then rounded to next width. This equals number of widths required. Widths required X's cut length divided by 36 equals ya

V115, V149

PLAIN FABRIC WITH LINING (lining recommended)

Finished length plus 30'' equals cut length. Pleat-to X's 3 divided by fabric width, rounded to next whole This equals widths required. Widths required X's cut length divided by 36 equals yardage.

PRINTED FABRICS WITH LINING

Finished length plus 30'' divided by repeat, then rounded to higher whole number (if number is frac Whole number X's repeat equals cut length. Pleat-to X's 3 divided by fabric width, rounded to next whole This equals width required. Widths required X's cut length divided by 36 equals yardage.

V118, V119, V120, V150, V151, V152, V153, V154

These are beautiful valances, but difficult to make. Not all workrooms can do them. If your workroom them, its best to have your workroom also figure out the yardage requirements.

V121, V122, V123,

PLAIN FABRIC UNLINED (recommended)

Finished length X's 3 equals cut length. Pleat-to X's two and a half, divided by fabric width, rounded whole width equals widths required. Widths required X's cut length divided by 36 equals yardage. Fo add one extra yard every 5 feet for jabots, and add 3 yards extra for each cascade. For valance V123 c should be self lined. If you want to use lining on these valances, then lining amount equals yardage a

V124, V139 (SEE CHAPTER: FABRIC SHADES)

V125, V126, V127, V128, V140

PLAIN FABRIC WITH LINING

Finished length plus 10'' equals cut length. Pleat-to X's two and one half, divided by fabric width, re to next whole width equals widths required. Widths X's cut length divided by 36 equals yardage.

PLAIN FABRIC SELF LINED

Finished length X's two plus 10'' equals cut length. Pleat-to X's two and one half, divided by fabric width, r to next whole width. This equals widths required. Widths X's cut length divided by 36 equals yarda

PRINTED FABRICS WITH LINING (lining recommended)

Finished length plus 10'' divided by repeat, then rounded to higher whole number (if number is frac Whole number X's repeat equals cut length. Pleat-to X's two and a half divided by fabric width, rou next whole width. Width X's cut length divided by 36 equals yardage.

ADDITIONAL INFORMATION

We have attempted to follow the industry standards with the above information. Your workroom may cut lengths, and other requirements. Its best to check with your workroom to see if above formulas are acc

Generally if you want to add lining to above valances then lining amount equals yardage amount.

Swag with Asymetric Cascades

Boxed Swag Valance

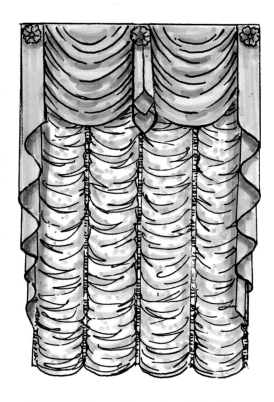

Swags Over Austrian Shade

Swag with Rosettes & Bow in Middle

Draped Swag with
Contrasting Lining

Swag with Lifted Center
& Cascading Tails

Double Swagged Valance

Single Swag with Rosettes

S65

rmal Swags & Cascades

S67

Swags & Rosettes

S69

Swag with Large Ties in Corners

S71

Gathered Swag

41

SC10

SC

SC20

SC25

SC30

SC35

Illustrations by Bonnie Glasser, New York, NY

SC40

SC45

SC50

SC55

SC60

trations by Bonnie Glasser, New York, NY

S79

Swag & Cascades with Ruffle
over Balloon Shade

S81

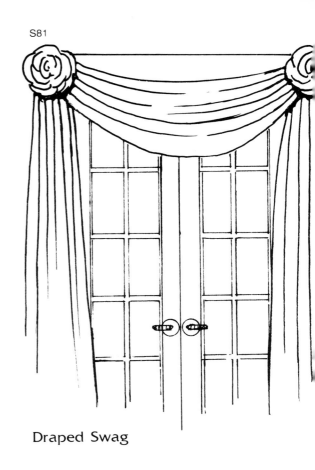

Draped Swag

S83

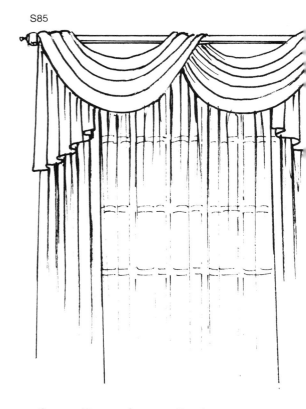

Swags & Jabots over Lace Panels

S85

Swag Draped over Rod

44

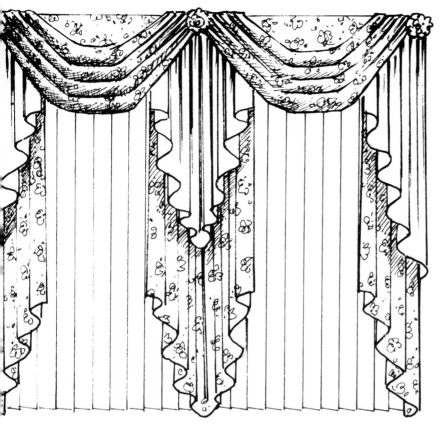

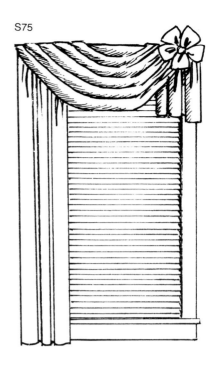

S75

Swag with Rosette &
Asymmetric Cascades

ble Swag with Plain Cascades over Print

S77

Swags & Cascades over Bay Window with French Doors

45

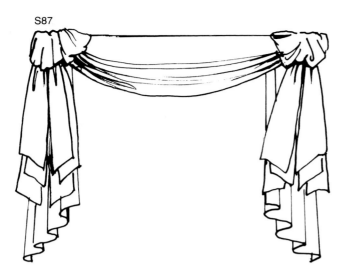

Swag and Cascade with Ties

Swag with Rosettes & Casca

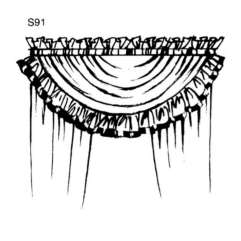

Ruffled Swag over Tie-backs

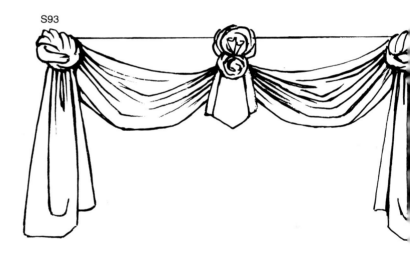

Double Swag with Rosettes & Cascades

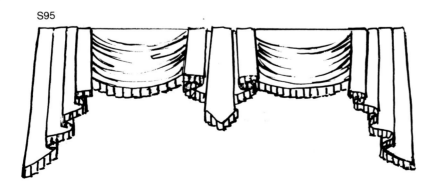

Double Swag with Cascades & Pleated Edge

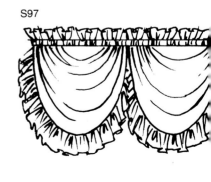

Ruffled Balloon Swag

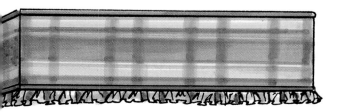

Cornice Box with Ruffle on Bottom

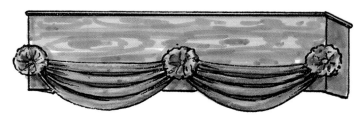

Cornice Box with Swag & Rosettes

Cornice Box with Shirred & Flat Panels

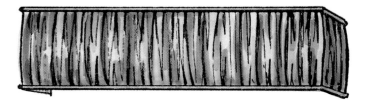

Shirred Cornice Box

Cornice Box with Pleated Fabric in Middle

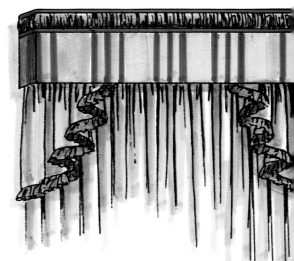

Cornice Box with Shirred Top Band
& Ruffled Cascades

Cornice box with Band at Bottom

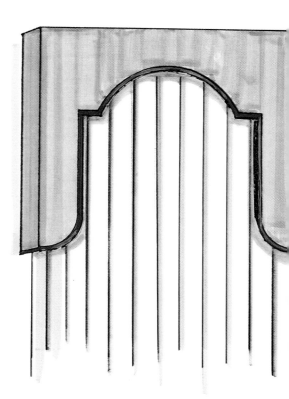

Shaped Cornice Box with Verticals

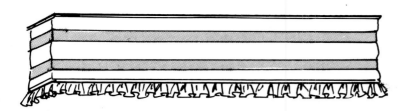

Cornice Box with Double Banding & Ruffle

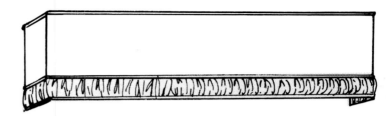

Shirred Bottom

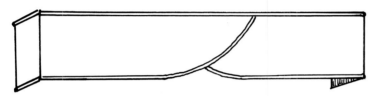

Special Welting Effect

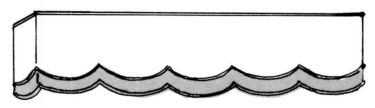

Scallop Bottom with Banding

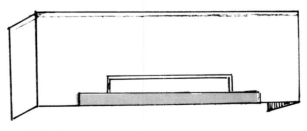

Fabric Insert

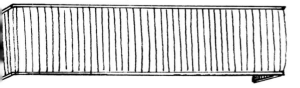

Pleated Box   2″ Pleated Box

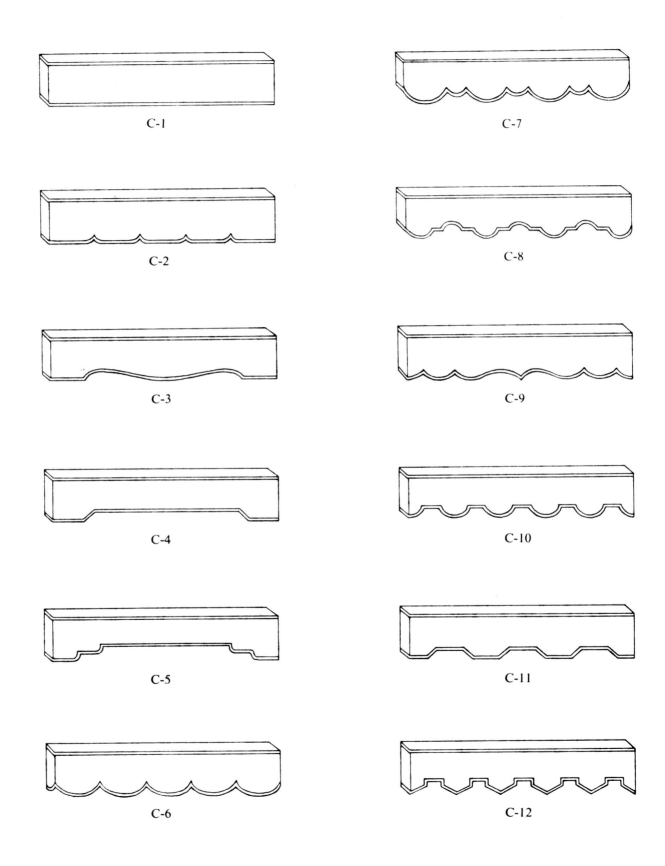

C-1

C-7

C-2

C-8

C-3

C-9

C-4

C-10

C-5

C-11

C-6

C-12

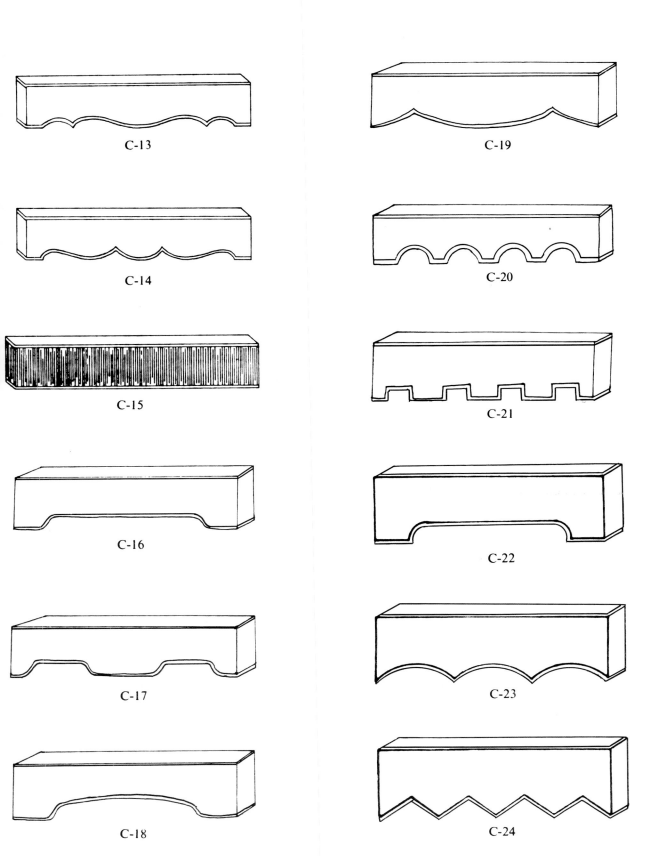

C-13

C-19

C-14

C-20

C-15

C-21

C-16

C-22

C-17

C-23

C-18

C-24

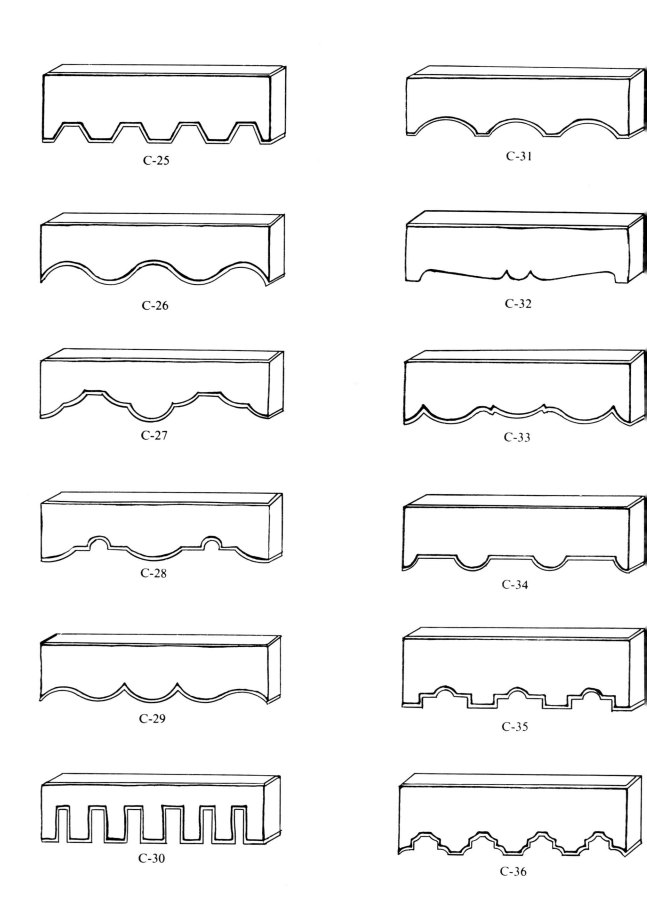

C-25

C-31

C-26

C-32

C-27

C-33

C-28

C-34

C-29

C-35

C-30

C-36

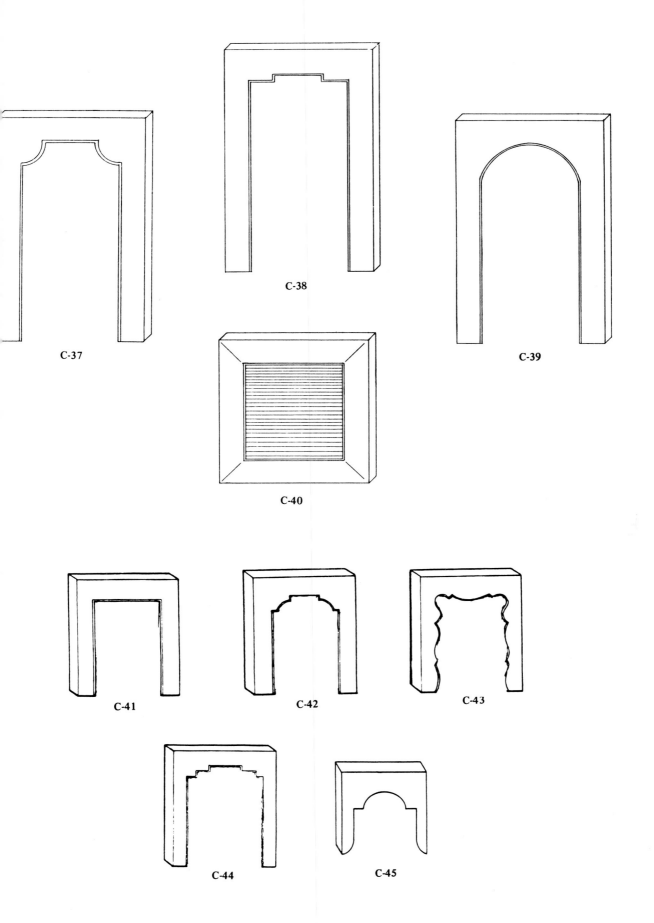

C-38

C-37

C-39

C-40

C-41

C-42

C-43

C-44

C-45

51

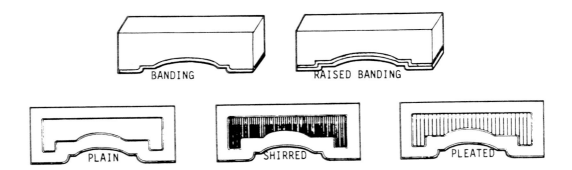

BANDING   RAISED BANDING

PLAIN   SHIRRED   PLEATED

General Information

The cornices are padded with polyester fiberfill and constructed of wood.

Non-directional and solid fabrics should be railroaded to eliminate seams. Matching welting is standard on all cornices and is applied to the top and bottom edges. Coordinating colors for welting has a more dramatic effect.

When ordering cornices to fit tight applications (i.e. wall to wall, bay windows), be sure to measure at the elevation of this installation. "Exact outside face measurement - wall to wall installation". Allow 1″ for clearance.

Measuring:

Measure drapery rod from end bracket to end bracket and add four inches for rod clearance and cornice returns. Six (6″) returns are needed when mounted over a single rod and eight (8″) returns when mounted over a double rod.

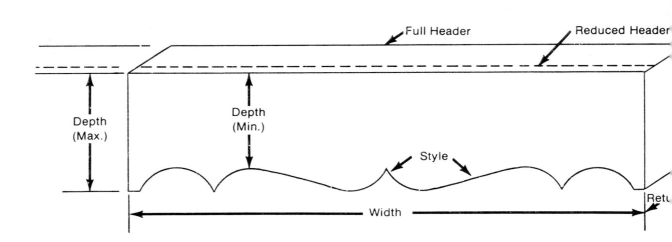

Cloud Shade with Bows at Top

Cloud Shade gathered on a pole
with ruffled upper edge

Balloon Shade

Balloon Shade with Shirred
Cornice Box

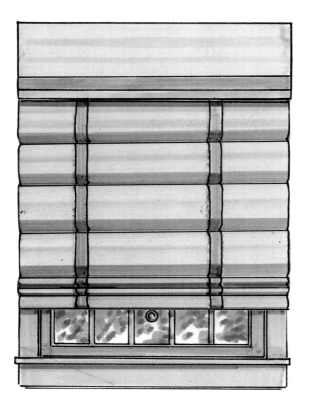

Roman Shade with Valance

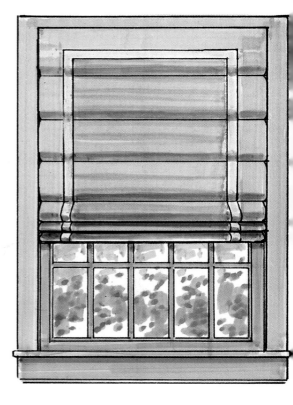

Roman Shade with Banding

Continental Cloud with Ruffles

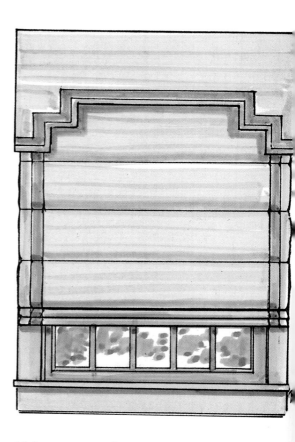

Valance over Roman Shade

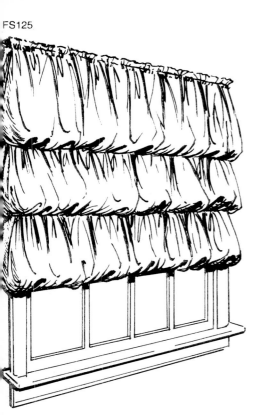

Tiered Cloud Shade

Cloud Shade with optional
Ruffled Bottom

Arched Top Cloud Shade

Bottom arched Balloon Shade

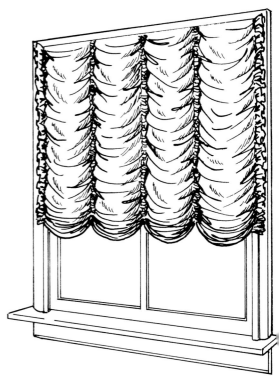

Cloud Shade Gathered on a Pole
with Ruffle at the top

Triple Fullness Fabric in Softly
Scalloped Panels distinguish
the Austrian Shade

FS102

FS102VAL

Cloud Shade with Four Inch Shirring
at top to give a Smocked Look

Shirred Cloud Shade with
matching Valance

Inverted Pleats & a Pouffed Bottom Edge characterize the elegant Balloon Shade

Pleated Balloon Shade with Matching Valance

FS113

FS123

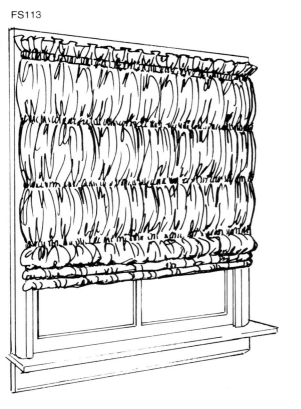

Fabric Gathered Triple Fullness on Horizontal Rods for a full but Tailored Look

Swagged Balloon Shirred on Continental Rod over Mini Blind

The dramatic Accordian Look
is created by rows of Mini-pleats

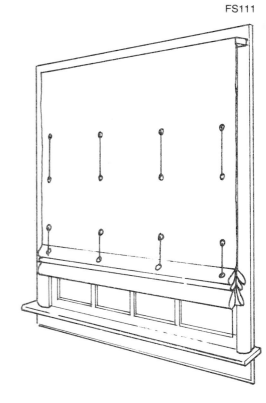

Brass Grommets & Front Cording
give a Nautical Look to this Shade

A Flat, simple Roman Shade that
draws up into graceful Folds when
raised

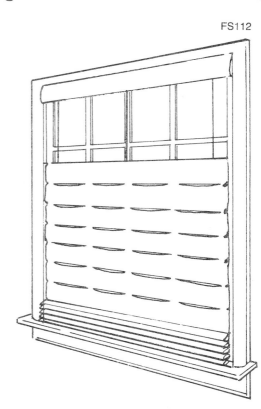

A Cord at each edge gives
needed support to this
Bottom-up Shade

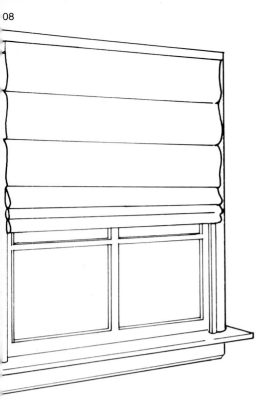

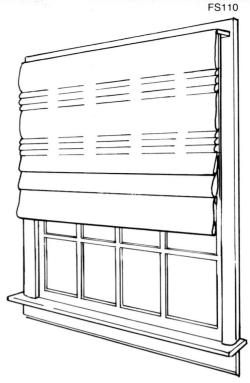

Distinctive Horizontal Pleating makes this
a very popular & versatile Roman Shade

Alternate Groups of Mini-pleats
with Single Panels gives this
blind a striking look all its own

Soft Overlapping Folds
create a Cascading Effect
on this Roman Shade

Alternating Large & Small Pleats
form a Repeating Pattern
on this Roman Shade

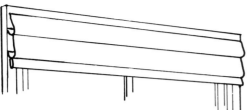

FSVAL1

This Valance has Soft
Folds & No Returns.

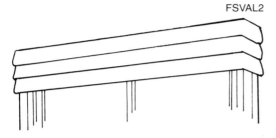

FSVAL2

For a more finished look, Soft
Folds wrap around the sides of
this Roman Valance

FS12

Soft Mini-fold Roman Shade

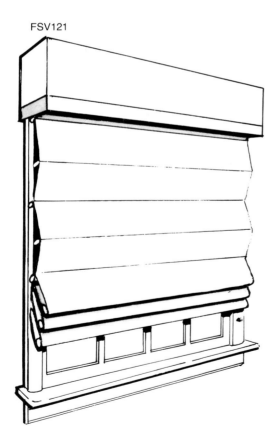

FSV121

Roman Shade with Valance
Overlapping

FS10

This very simple Roman Shade
flat when down & draws up in
graceful folds when raised

Measuring Instructions

Inside Installation

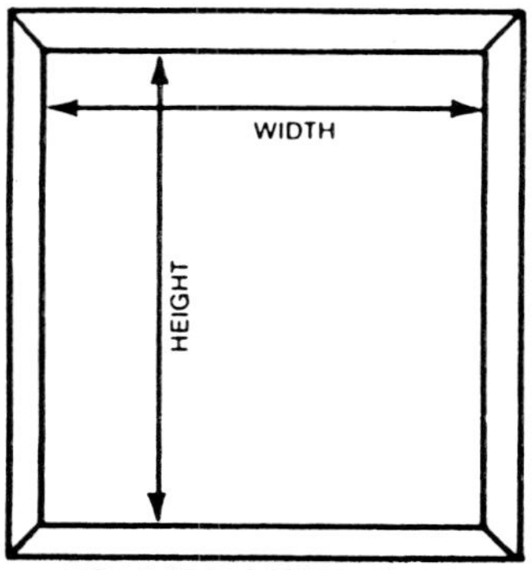

INSIDE OR RECESSED MOUNT

Measure width of window at the top, center and window, and use narrowest measurement when order- fy on order form if inside clearance has been made. If nce has been allowed factory will deduct ¼" from dth.

: Measure height of window from top of opening to top allowance is made for length.

Outside Installation

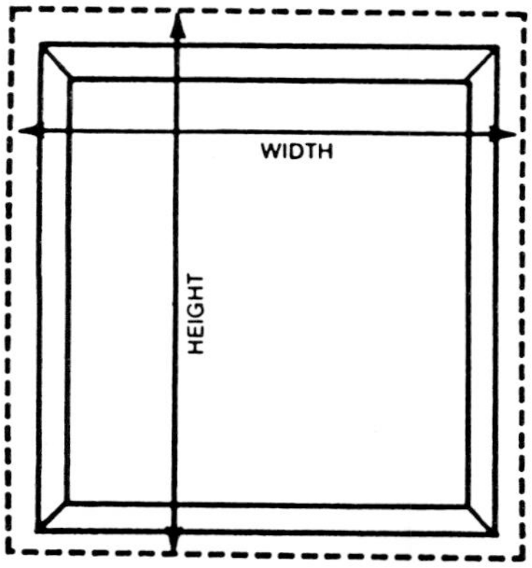

OUTSIDE OR WALL MOUNT

A. Width: Measure exact width of area to be covered. It is recommended that shades extend past actual window opening by 2" on each side. Furnish finished shade width, no allowances will be made.

B. Length: Measure length of area to be covered, allowing a minimum of 2½" at top of window to accomodate headerboard and brackets. (At this time you may want to take into consideration stackage of shades and allow for this in your length measurement.) Furnish finished shade length, no allowance will be made.

ALL INSTALLATIONS

. Specify right or left cord position. If no cord position is indicated, cords will be corded to right hand side.

. Specify cord length (length of cord needed for easy reach, when shade is completely down). If no specification is made, cord length will be approximately ⅓ length of shade.

. For Pole Cloud, Cloud, Balloon, Austrian™ and Aspen™ shades, specify if length given is high or low point of pouff.

Square Footage Chart

SHADE WIDTH
in inches

24	30	36	42	48	54	60	66	72	78	84	90	96	102	108	114	120	126	132	138	144
10	10	10	10	10	11¼	12½	13¾	15	16¼	17½	18¾	20	21¼	22½	23¾	25	26¼	27½	28¾	30
10	10	10	10½	12	13½	15	16½	18	19½	21	22½	24	25½	27	28½	30	31½	33	34½	36
10	10	10½	12¼	14	15¾	17½	19¼	21	22¾	24½	26¼	28	29¾	31½	33¼	35	36¾	38½	40¼	42
10	10	12	14	16	18	20	22	24	26	28	30	32	34	36	38	40	42	44	46	48
10	11¼	13½	15¾	18	20¼	22½	24¾	27	29¼	31½	33¾	36	38¼	40½	42¾	45	47¼	49½	51¾	54
10	12½	15	17½	20	22½	25	27½	30	32½	35	37½	40	42½	45	47½	50	52½	55	57½	60
11	13¾	16½	19¼	22	24¾	27½	30¼	33	35¾	38½	41¼	44	46¾	49½	52¼	55	57¾	60½	63¼	66
12	15	18	21	24	27	30	33	36	39	42	45	48	51	54	57	60	63	66	69	72
13	16¼	19½	22¾	26	29¼	32½	35¾	39	42¼	45½	48¾	52	55¼	58½	61¾	65	68¼	71½	74¾	78
14	17½	21	24½	28	31½	35	38½	42	45½	49	52½	56	59½	63	66½	70	73½	77	80½	84
15	18¾	22½	26¼	30	33¾	37½	41¼	45	48¾	52½	56¼	60	63¾	67½	71¼	75	78¾	82½	86¼	90
16	20	24	28	32	36	40	44	48	52	56	60	64	68	72	76	80	84	88	92	96
17	21¼	25½	29¾	34	38¼	42½	46¾	51	55¼	59½	63¾	68	72¼	76½	80¾	85	89¼	93½	97¾	102
18	22½	27	31½	36	40½	45	49½	54	58½	63	67½	72	76½	81	85½	90	94½	99	103½	108
9	23¾	28½	33¼	38	42¾	47½	52¼	57	61¾	66½	71¼	76	80¾	85½	90¼	95	99¾	104½	109¼	114
20	25	30	35	40	45	50	55	60	65	70	75	80	85	90	95	100	105	110	115	120
21	26¼	31½	36¾	42	47¼	52½	57¾	63	68¼	73½	78¾	84	89¼	94½	99¾	105	110¼	115½	120¾	126
22	27½	33	38½	44	49½	55	60½	66	71½	77	82½	88	93½	99	104½	110	115½	121	126½	132
23	28¾	34½	40¼	46	51¾	57½	63¼	69	74¾	80½	86¼	92	97¾	103½	109¼	115	120¾	126½	132¼	138
24	30	36	42	48	54	60	66	72	78	84	90	96	102	108	114	120	126	132	138	144

Yardage Requirements

FS100 • FS101 • FS104 • FS106 • FS107 • FS108
FS110 • FS111 • FS112 • FS121 • FSV124

1. Width of Shade:
Measure width of area to be covered by shade. Figure how many widths of material across area you wil
When more than one width is needed, estimate full width only. One width will cover 4'' less than actual, width o

2. Length of Shade:
Measure length of area to be covered by shade and proceed below to appropriate design:
FS106, FS111. Multiply length of shade by 1.25, and add 14'' for top and bottom hems.
FS108. Multiply lengths x 1.33 and add 14'' for top and bottom hems.
FS100. Multiply length by 1.5, and add 14'' for top and bottom hems.
FS104. Multiply length x 1.75, and add 14'' for top and bottom hems.
FS101, FS110. Multiply length by 2.0, and add 14'' for top and bottom hems.
FS107. Multiply length x 2.65, and add 14'' for top and bottom hems.

3. Multiply Widths x Lengths = Fabric Required in inches. Divide by 36'' for yardage.*
   * **Important:** when working with a fabric that has a pattern repeat, add one repeat per width of fabric.

FS102 • FS102V • FS103 • FS109 • FS109V • FS113
FS117 • FS123 • FS125 • FSA126 • FSA127
(We suggest wrinkle resistant fabric)

1. Width of Shade or Valance:
Measure width of area to be covered by shade or valance. Multiply by three. Divide this number by width o
this equals number of widths required. When more than one width is required estimate full width only.

2. Length of Shade or Valance:
Measure length of area to be covered by shade or valance.
FS102, FS103, FS109, FS113: length of shade plus 36'' for hem and fullness.

3. Multiply Widths x Lengths = Fabric Required in inches. Divide by 36'' for yardage.*
   * **Important:** when working with a fabric that has a pattern repeat, add one repeat per width of fabric.
   • **FS117.** Add ½ yard per linear foot for ruffle.
   • **FS109V, FS102V.** add 1 yard per 1½ linear foot for valance.

• FS115 •
(We suggest wrinkle resistant fabric)

1. Width of Shade or Valance:
Measure width of area to be covered by shade or valance. Multiply x 1.65. Divide this number by width o
this equals number of widths required. When more than one width is required estimate full width only.

2. Length of Shade or Valance.
Measure length of area to be covered by shade or valance and proceed to appropriate design:
FS115: length of shade x 3.

3. Multiply Widths x Length = Fabric Required in Inches. Divide by 36'' for yardage*
   *** Important:** when working with a fabric that has a pattern repeat, add 1 repeat per width of fabric.

Bow Tied Ruffled Tie-backs

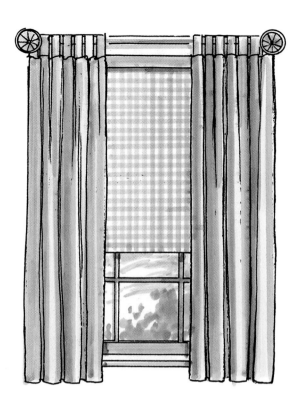

Tab-top Curtains on Dec. Rod

Ruffled Tie-backs over Balloon Shade

Multiple Tie-backs Shirred Between
Top & Bottom Continental Rods

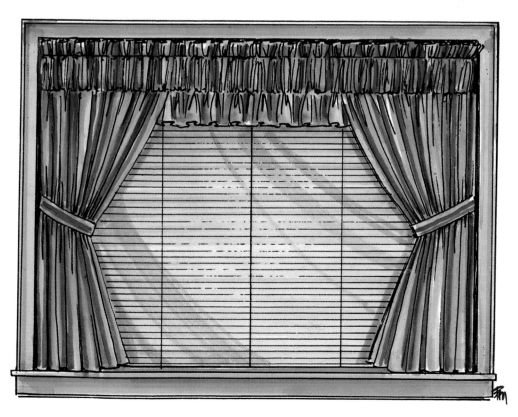

Tie-back Curtains on Continental Rod
with Top Ruffle & Center Sleeve Valance

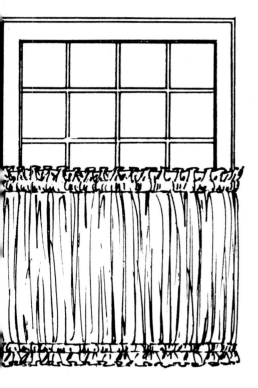

fe Curtains Shirred top-to-bottom
tween Two Rods

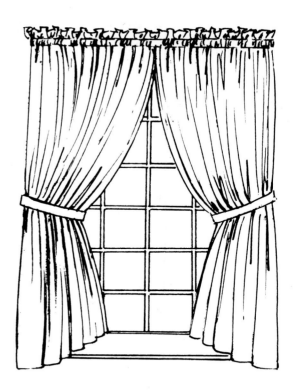

Tied-back Curtains Gathered on Rod

rapery Gathered on a Dec. Rod &
ied Back with Large Bows

Austrian Shade with Ruffles

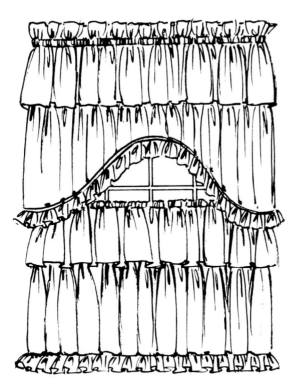

Cafe Curtains with Arched Top & Valance

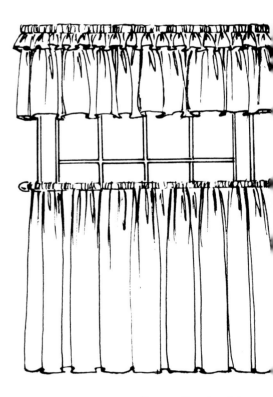

Cafe Curtains on Brass Rod with Gathered Valance

Traditional Swag with Mini-blind

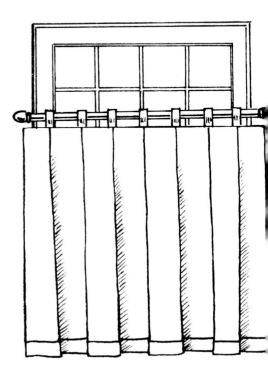

Pleated Tab-top Cafe Curtains on Brass Rod

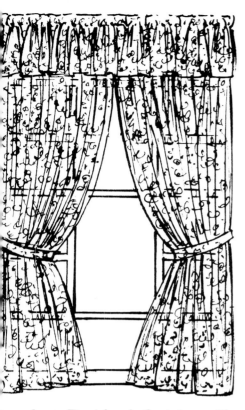

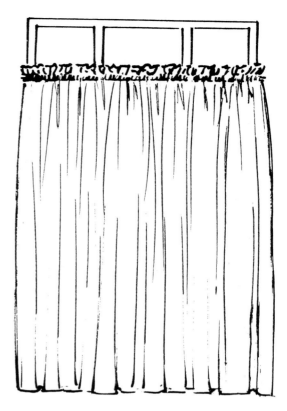

heer Lace Tied-back Curtains with
athered Valance

Shirred Cafe Curtain on High Rod

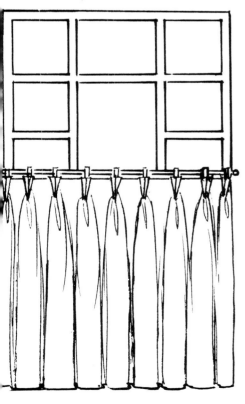

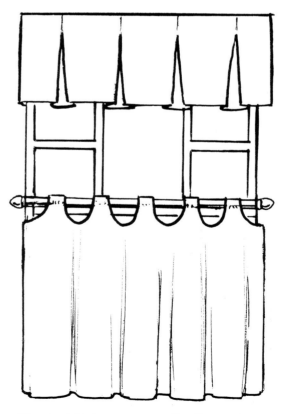

afe Curtains with French Pleated
ps on Rings

Pleated Valance over Scalloped
Cafe Curtains

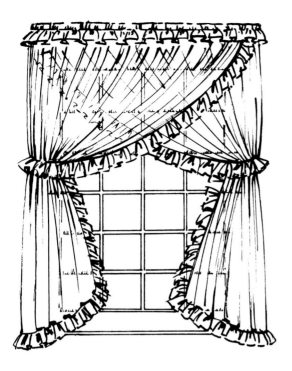

Priscilla Curtains with Ruffles

Valance on Brass Dec. Rod over Tie
back Curtains with Ruffles

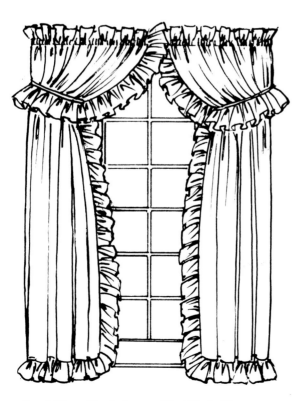

Rod-Top Curtains with High Ties
and Large Ruffles

Priscilla Curtains with Continental To

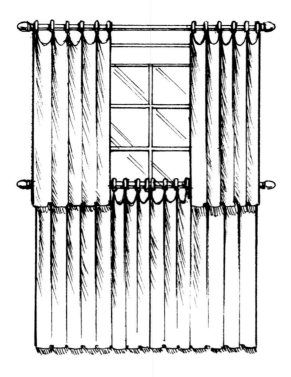

Double Cafe Curtains with Scalloped
Top on Brass Rod

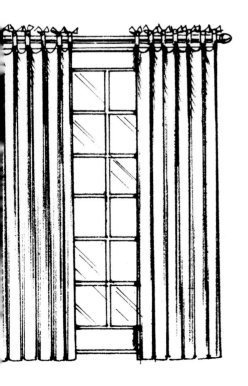

-tied Curtains on Brass Dec. Rod

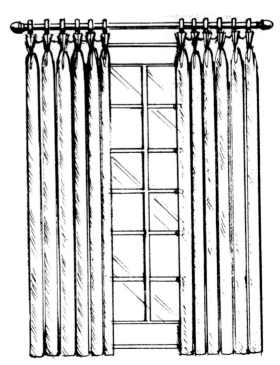

French Pleated Curtains with Scalloped
Heading on Brass Dec. Rod

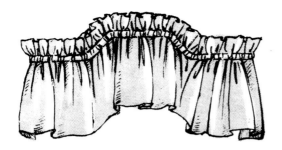

Arched Valance

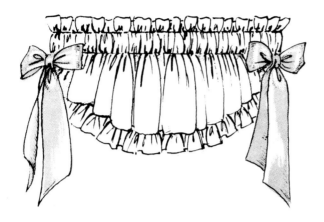

Valance with Bows

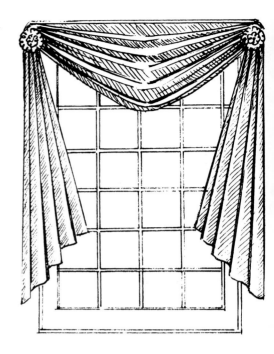

Alternate — Traditional Swag

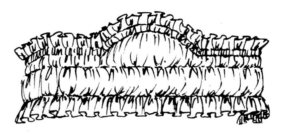

Cathedral Top Valance
on Continental Rod

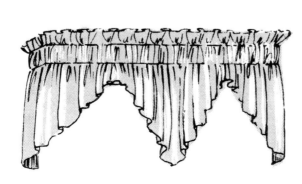

Double Arched Valance on Continental Rod

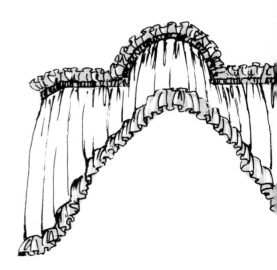

Cathedral Top Valance with tapere

STRAIGHT PLAIN
STYLE No. 1

TAPERED PLAIN
STYLE No. 2

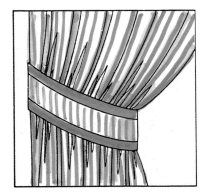

STRAIGHT WITH BANDING
STYLE No. 3

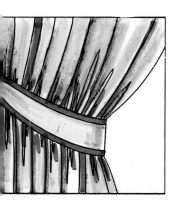

ERED WITH WELT CORD
STYLE No. 4

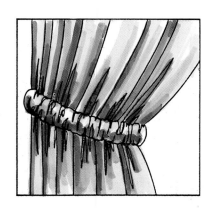

SHIRRED JUMBO WELT CORD
STYLE No. 5

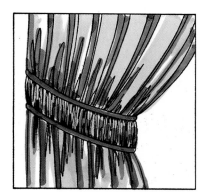

STRAIGHT SHIRRED
WITH WELT CORD
STYLE No. 6

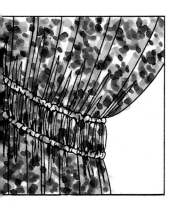

STRAIGHT SHIRRED
STYLE No. 7

BRAIDED
STYLE No. 8

STRAIGHT WITH ROSETTE
STYLE No. 9

**STRAIGHT WITH BOW
STYLE No. 10**

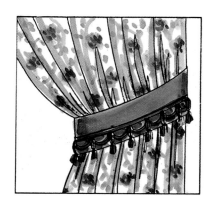

**STRAIGHT WITH FRINGE
STYLE No. 11**

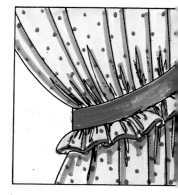

STRAIGHT WITH RUFF
STYLE No. 12

**RUFFLED
STYLE No. 13**

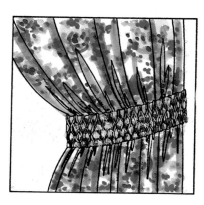

**NEW SHIRRED LOOK
STYLE No. 14**

FORMAL TIE WITH CASC
STYLE No. 15

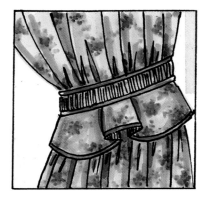

**SHIRRED TIE WITH PLEAT
STYLE No. 16**

**DOUBLE RUFFLED TIE
STYLE No. 17**

BOX PLEATED TIE WITH WE
STYLE No. 18

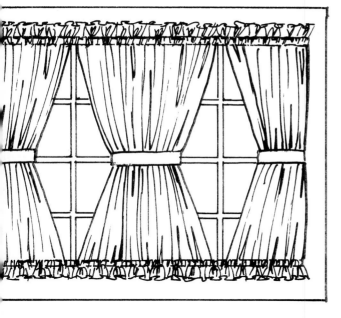

Double Diamond Effect–
Rod Top & Bottom

mond Effect–
Top & Bottom

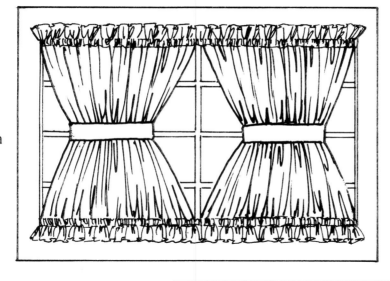

Double Rod Top & Bottom

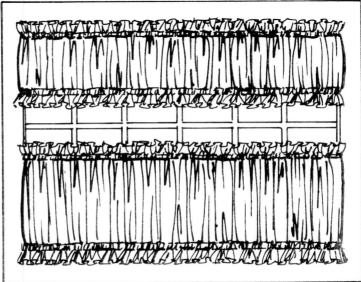

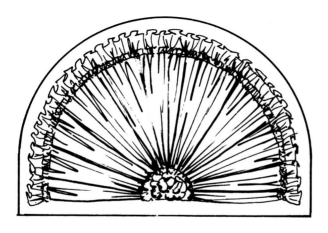

Sunburst

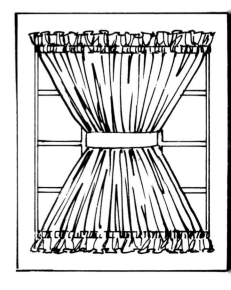

Hourglass – Rod Top & Bottom

Diamond – Rod Top & Bottom

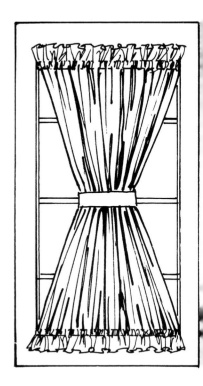

Hourglass Rod Top & Bott

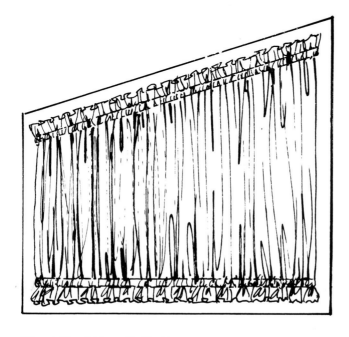

Slant Rod Top & Bottom

ACCESSORIES

ILLOW SHAM · PLAIN

LLOW SHAM · QUILTED

SHAM WITH WELT CORDING

FLANGED SHAM

YARDAGE AMOUNTS

PILLOWS

YARDAGE AMOUNTS FOR ONE PILLOW:
(45" – 54" fabric)

	12" – 15"	16" – 18"	20" – 24"
KNIFE EDGE PILLOW	1/2 yd	3/4 yd	1 yd

OPTIONS

	12" – 15"	16" – 18"	20" – 24"
1/4" welt	1/4 yd	1/4 yd	1/4 yd
1" welt	1/2 yd	1/2 yd	3/4 yd
3" – 4" ruffle (54" fabric)	1 yd	1 yd	1 1/2 yd

CHAIR CUSHIONS:
(45" – 54" fabric)

	16" or smaller
Body of cushion	1/2 yd
1/4 welt & ties	1/2 yd
Ruffle (up to 3")	1 yd

DIRECTOR CHAIR COVER: 1 yd

BOLSTERS:

	36"	45"	54"
36"	1 1/2 yds	1 1/2 yds	1 yd
39"	2 yds	1 1/2 yds	1 yd
60"	2 yds	2 yds	2 yds
72"	2 1/2 yds	2 yds	2 yds

TABLESKIRTS:

Yardage amounts — If total diameter of skirt is greater than width of fabric, the length of fabric needed is double the diameter of skirt. If total diameter of skirt is as much or less than width of fabric, the length of fabric is needed is one diameter measurement of skirt.

******ADD 1 REPEAT OF PATTERN FOR PRINTED FABRICS******

BED COVER STYLES

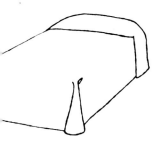

THROW

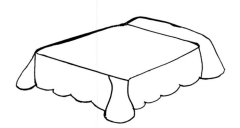

SCALLOPED

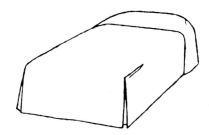

THROW — FITTED

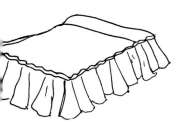

**QUILTED TOP
SHIRRED DROP**

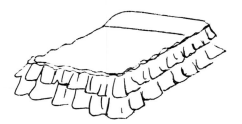

**QUILTED TOP
DOUBLE SHIRRED DROP**

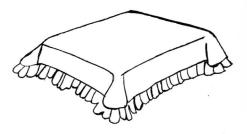

THROW WITH RUFFLE

ILTED COMFORLET

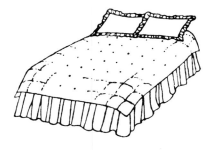

TUFTED COMFORTED
(Standard Sizes Only)

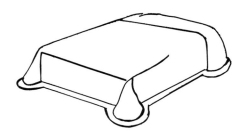

1″ CORD

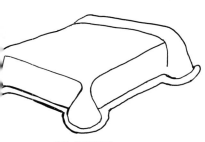

2″ CORD

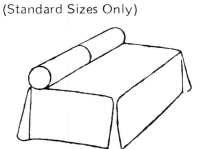

STUDIO COUCH COVER

DAYBED TUFTED COMFORTER
(Standard Twin Only)

The standard drop for bedspreads is 21″ For coverlets and comforters, the standard drop is 12½″.

Custom Dust Ruffles are fabricated in three styles: **SHIRRED, TAILORED** or **BOX PLEATED**.

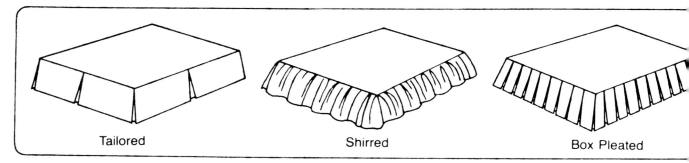

Tailored   Shirred   Box Pleated

HOW TO MEASURE: (Exact measurements are necessary)
- A -- Length of Boxsprings
- B -- Width of Boxsprings
- C -- Drop from top of Boxsprings to floor

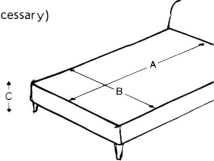

UPHOLSTERED HEADBOARDS

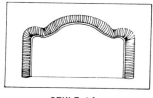

STYLE #1

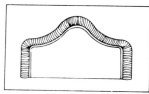

STYLE #2

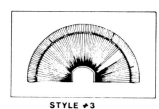

STYLE #3

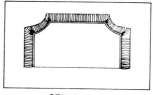

STYLE #4

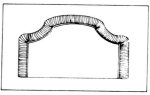

STYLE #5

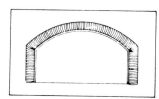

STYLE #6

STYLE #7

DIMENSIONS

STYLE	TWIN	FULL	QUEEN	KING
1,2,5,7	41W X 51H	56W X 53H	62W X 55H	81W X 56H
3	41W X 53H	56W X 55H	62W X 57H	81W X 57H
4,6	41W X 49H	56W X 49H	62W X 51H	81W X 53H

	36"	48"	54"
Twin	12 yards	8 yards	8 yards
Full	12 yards	12 yard	8 yards
Queen	15 yards	12 yards	12 yards
King	15 yards	12 yards	12 yards

Additional Yardage Requirements: For Prints—Add 1 yard
Additional Yardage Optional Features
For Reverse Sham—Add 3 yards   For Jumbo Cord—Add 2 yards

COMFORTER YARDAGE

Twin, Full, Queen—7 yds./side
King—11 yds./side

		36"	45"	54"
Twin	36"	1 1/2 yards	1 1/2 yards	1 yard
Full	39"	2 yards	1 1/2 yards	1 yard
Queen	60"	2 yards	2 yards	2 yards
King	72"	2 1/2 yards	2 yards	2 yard

Add 1 Repeat of Pattern For Prints.

PILLOW SHAMS

1 1/2 yards—Ruffles add 1 1/2 yards

DUSTERS

	36" Fabric		45" or Wider	
	Tailored	Shirred or 4" Box Pleat	Tailored	Shirred or 4" Box Pleat
Twin	3 3/4 yards	8 1/2 yards	2 3/4 yards	6 1/2 yards
Full	3 3/4 yards	8 1/2 yards	2 3/4 yards	7 yards
Queen	4 1/2 yards	10 yards	3 yards	7 1/2 yards
King	4 1/2 yards	10 yards	3 yards	7 1/2 yards

GENERAL INFORMATION

Bedspreads are made to fit following standard bed sizes.

Twin	39 x 75
Full	54 x 75
Queen	60 x 80
King	72 x 84

Round Bedspreads 7', 8' (Made to your measurements)

STANDARD DROPS

Bedspreads 21"
Coverlets 12"
Dusters 14"
Pillow Tuck 15"
Drop over 22" Add:

BOW KNOT

LEAF

BOW KNOT

STRAIGHT DIAMOND

POPPY

SHELL

CHINESE

CHEVRON

PAGODA

SCROLL

VINE

HERITAGE

VERMICILLI

ZIGZAG SQUARE

CLOUDS

LA PLUME

ZIGZAG DIAMOND

OUTLINE QUILT

BUTTERFLY

CHANNEL

Notes